NEW YORK JUSTICE

ISBN13: 978-1942500-28-5

BOULEVARD BOOKS

The New Face of Publishing

www.BoulevardBooks.org

New York Justice

My 40-Year Courtroom Journey from Rookie Prosecutor to Veteran Criminal Trial Judge

By Judge Joel M. Goldberg (ret.)

DEDICATION

This book is lovingly dedicated to

my wife, Eleanor, and my son, Jason.

ACKNOWLEDGEMENTS

Because this book is based on my 44-year career as an Assistant District Attorney and a Judge, both the book and my career would not have been possible without the people I worked with over all those years who helped me in so many different ways.

In my years in the District Attorney' Office, I worked with hundreds of other Assistant District Attorneys as a colleague and a supervisor in my various assignments. I would like to acknowledge them all, but special mention should be made of those in Executive and Bureau Chief positions who were role models, mentors, and so encouraging to me: District Attorneys Eugene Gold and Elizabeth Holtzman; Executive Assistant District Attorneys William Donnino; Zachery Carter; and Barbara Underwood; Bureau and Deputy Bureau Chiefs Roger Adler; Michael Belson; Helman Brook; Paul DeMartini; Vincent Fay; Sheldon Greenberg; Gordon Haesloop; Michael Halberstam, Robert Keating; Albert Koch; Richard Laskey; Richard Mischel; Edward Rappaport; Barry Schreiber William Siegel; Arnold Taub; and Alan Trachtman. I also wish to acknowledge my Supervising Criminal Court Judge William Miller and Supreme Court Administrative Judges: Ronald Aiello; Matthew D'Emic; Neil Firetog; Barry Kamins; Michael Pesce; Ann Phau; and Staten Island Supervising Supreme Court Judge Wally Sangiorgio.

My "court family" deserves special mention: my law clerks Charmaine Morrison-Black; Michael Polizutto; and Ernest Hambrock in particular whose trial notes during the period covered in this book were invaluable; court clerks Erik DeLucca; Michael Raphael; and Barry Winker; and secretaries Joyce Kuhne and Francesca Traversa, all of whom made my work easier, better, and were unfailingly patient with me every day.

CONTENTS

INTRODUCTION

In January of 2016 due to reaching the mandatory judicial retirement age of 70, I retired after 28 years as a judge in New York City. For most of those years, I was assigned to Brooklyn where I handled all varieties of criminal cases. Brooklyn was also where I had previously spent 16 years as an Assistant District Attorney, so by the time I retired I had not only "seen it all" in the criminal law field, I also had done it all too. My goal in writing this memoir is not only to capture some of the highlights of my career, but also to convey a sense of both what it was like to be a young Assistant District Attorney in the 1970's as well as provide a sampling of the types of criminal trials that take place every day in our City's courts. This memoir is written for non-lawyers, so some basic legal concepts are explained for their benefit.

In reviewing my files to decide what trials to discuss, I began with the most recent ones starting in the year 2015. By the time I went back to 2008, I realized that there were a sufficient number of trials to convey a general picture of the almost 500 felony trials I presided over between 1992 and 2015. Therefore, I decided that for purposes of this volume, I would discuss only one pre-2008 trial, which was a murder case I presided over while sitting on Staten Island. I should note that my experiences as an Assistant District Attorney and as a judge were not particularly unique. Literally thousands of Assistant District Attorneys have tried the types of criminal cases I tried and almost as many have argued the types of criminal appeals I argued, although it is a much rarer occurrence, due to the specialized nature of appellate practice, for one person to have done both trial and appellate work.

As for my experience as a judge, most judges assigned to try felony cases have tried the types of cases I tried. While I certainly have tried my share, there are judges who have tried more cases, or more complex cases, or more highly publicized cases. There may even be judges who have even enjoyed doing this as much as I did, notwithstanding all the worries and wrestling with the difficult decisions that come with the job of being a trial judge. I was an Assistant District Attorney in Brooklyn for 16 years. For 12 of those years, I held supervisory or executive positions which limited my opportunity to be in court with my own cases. After four years in the Office trying cases and arguing appeals, I was promoted to the position of trial supervisor in the Narcotics Bureau and subsequently to supervisory positions in the Criminal Court Bureau, Supreme Court Trial Bureau, Appeals Bureau, Grand Jury Bureau, and ultimately to Deputy Chief Assistant District Attorney from which position I left the Office to become a judge.

What I did as a supervisor and an executive in the Office was important and professionally fulfilling, but, because it would involve discussions of how I interacted with other people, both in and out of the Office, it is not really the subject for the type of memoire I want to write. It also would not be particularly interesting to those who do not know the other people involved. Therefore, I am omitting this not insubstantial portion of my legal life. While an Assistant District Attorney, I was appointed to be a Judge of the New York City Criminal Court in June of 1987 by Mayor Edward I. Koch. The appointment was to fill a judicial vacancy created by the election of a Criminal Court Judge to a higher judicial office. The vacant position had approximately five years left on its 10-year term, meaning that after that term expired in 1992, I would have to be re-appointed by the next Mayor in order to keep my job.

Mayor Koch had created a policy of removing politics from his judicial appointments. His selections were based on a "merit selection" screening process by a non-partisan committee of lawyers which sent three names to the Mayor for each vacancy. The Mayor and his executive staff conducted the final interviews. I was fortunate enough to have had a second opportunity to interview with Mayor Koch in 1987 after previously, in 1983, going through the series of multiple interviews involved in the process but not making the final cut. It was disappointing, to say the least, when a few days after the 1983 interview with the Mayor, his Criminal Justice Coordinator, and the chair of his Judicial Screening Committee, I received a telephone call telling me that I was not selected. Naturally, after that call I looked back on the interview with the Mayor and wondered if I had answered any of the interview questions differently whether it would have made a difference.

By the time of the second interview in 1987, I was Deputy Chief Assistant District Attorney and had also worked closely with District Attorney, Elizabeth Holtzman and had her support for the appointment. I am sure both of these factors made the difference.

Mayor Koch, as he was during the first interview, was cordial, actively involved in the questioning, and seemed sincerely committed to appointing judges who had proven legal ability in the criminal law field as well as common sense. His legacy of high quality judicial appointments over his 12-year term has made me proud to have been part of that group. As a Criminal Court Judge, I presided over cases involving misdemeanors and lesser charges such as shoplifting, simple assaults, intoxicated driving, possession of small amounts of drugs, and, literally, spitting on the sidewalk. Criminal Court Judges also handle arraignments of people arrested for both felonies and misdemeanors where bail decisions are made and the less serious cases are often "disposed of" by dismissals or guilty pleas. Due to the volume of arrests in New York City, these arraignments generally take place seven days a week in two court sessions running from 9:00 am to 1:00 am the next day. I was initially assigned to the Criminal Court in Queens for six months, and then I was assigned to Brooklyn. After sitting in Brooklyn Criminal Court steadily for three years, I was assigned to alternate every month between Brooklyn and Staten Island. Sitting on Staten Island where I lived made the commute to work much easier. However, this meant that I would be far more likely to encounter the defendants whose cases came before me.

Three examples come to mind: (1) My neighbor's teenage son was given a summons for drinking beer in public and his case came before me. It was hardly worth the time to bring in another judge to handle the case, because these cases, especially for young first-offenders, were routinely disposed of with a warning and a dismissal, although this case, due to my presiding, contained a component of additional embarrassment to the defendant and his mother; (2) while dining in a restaurant with my wife, I recognized our busboy as someone who had a pending case before me and, although nothing was said during the meal, on the way out he discreetly whispered to my wife, "say hello to the judge," and, (3) after I called road service to come to my house to jump start a car with a dead battery, the tow truck driver who came to my house turned out to be a defendant who had a pending case before me for, of all things, stealing a tow truck. Not only did he now know exactly where I lived, I had to decide how much to tip him.

In July of 1992, while still holding the office of Criminal Court Judge, I was assigned by the State Office of Court Administration to sit in the New York State Supreme Court as an Acting Supreme Court Justice. Then, as now, it was routine practice to supplement the existing contingent of elected Supreme Court Justices with experienced Criminal Court Judges. My elevation to the Supreme Court came as a surprise to me. There were a number of more experienced Criminal Court Judges who were well-qualified, and I had been a Criminal Court Judge for only five years. I attribute my expedited promotion to Supreme Court in 1992 to be the result of the professional relationship I had established in the late 1970's with the Administrative Judge in Brooklyn Supreme Court, Ronald Aiello, when he was Chief of the Homicide Bureau in the District Attorney's Office and I was in the Appeals Bureau. At that time, I had made myself available to the Assistant District Attorneys in the Homicide Bureau to help them with legal issues while they were on trial. I later became aware through the grapevine that Judge Aiello, without my knowing it, had lobbied the decision-makers in the Office of Court Administration to expedite my promotion to the Supreme Court where I remained for the next 23 years.

If I had not been administratively elevated to be an Acting Supreme Court Justice, I may never have had the opportunity to preside over felony cases, because I did not have the political connections necessary to obtain a political party's nomination for election to a Supreme Court judgeship. I remained an "Acting" Supreme Court Justice without having to engage in political activity of any kind. Rather than face an election or re-election, my only "campaign" was for Mayoral re-appointments to the Criminal Court which involved filling out application forms detailing my judicial activity and going through a series of interviews with various bar associations and the Mayor's Judicial Screening Committee, a non-partisan procedure that, after it was initiated by Mayor Koch, was continued by subsequent Mayors. Upon the expiration of my original term of office in November of 1992, I was re-appointed as a Criminal Court Judge by then Mayor David N. Dinkins for a full 10-year term, and then twice more re-appointed to 10-year terms in 2002 and 2012 by then Mayor Michael R. Bloomberg. It is my hope that this memoir will provide some insight into the judicial process.

PART I.   IN THE DISTRICT ATTORNEY'S OFFICE

Chapter 1. *MY START IN THE DA'S OFFICE*

"Are you a 'Regular' or a 'Reformer'? asked Brooklyn Assistant District Attorney Alex Singer when I met him in June of 1971 on my first day as a newly hired prosecutor in the Investigations Bureau of the Brooklyn District Attorney's Office. Even after the 1968 election of politically well-connected Brooklyn attorney Eugene Gold as District Attorney and his institution of non-political hiring, the Office was still populated with many Assistant District Attorneys who got their jobs the old-fashioned way, through political connections and Democratic Party politics. Alex was simply trying to find out where I stood and to whom I owed my job.

I told him I was neither, and that I got my job after responding to a notice posted on my law school's job placement bulletin board stating that the Brooklyn District Attorney's Office was seeking law school graduates to become Assistant District Attorneys.

Since 1968, under the leadership of District Attorney Gold, the Office began hiring law school graduates from around the country without regard to their political affiliation. The Office grew from less than 100 lawyers in 1968 (many of whom were excellent attorneys and dedicated public servants regardless of how they may have gotten their jobs) to over 300 in 1980 as the result of budget increases. During the time, the Office lost its political character and became nationally known for the quality of its legal team.

My hiring process began with the submission of my resume and an interview with two executive level Assistant District Attorneys, Edward Rappaport and Norman Rosen. I vividly recall being asked a series of hypothetical questions regarding how I would respond to various situations that might come up while working in the Office. For example, I was asked about my willingness to follow a supervisor's instructions as to how to proceed on a case even if I personally believed something else should be done, such as an instruction to prosecute a serious felony as a misdemeanor based on weak evidence of guilt in the case. I dutifully replied that I would defer to the supervisor's judgment based on my lack of experience, even though I might disagree with the decision.

The hypothetical questions then morphed into situations where the supervisor was asking me to do various things that could be considered unethical, such as telling the judge something that was not true or not disclosing facts about the case that would be helpful to the defendant. I essentially said that I would not do these things and, if I had no alternative, I would resign from the Office. After hypothetically quitting the job I was seeking several times during these questions, the interview concluded.

Somewhat rattled, I got up from my chair and turned to leave, but I could not remember which door of the well-paneled conference room was the exit. Of course, I chose the wrong door and walked into an adjoining office. Realizing I had no choice, I had to re-enter the conference room and say good-bye again to the amusement of my two interviewers.

Nevertheless, I was called back for an interview the following Saturday morning with District Attorney Gold and his Chief Assistant District Attorney, Elliott Golden. There were no hypothetical questions during that interview. At the conclusion of the interview, I was offered and accepted the job.

Chapter 2. *THE INVESTIGATIONS BUREAU*

I started in June of 1971 in the Brooklyn District Attorney's Office then located in the Municipal Building at 210 Joralemon Street. My first assignment was in the Investigations Bureau along with about ten other newly hired law school graduates. Our official title was "Criminal Law Investigator." We could not be designated Assistant District Attorneys (and receive a raise in annual salary from $9,800 to $11,000) until we were notified that we had passed the New York Bar Examination and became licensed to practice law.

One of our two main functions in the Investigations Bureau was handling investigations of citizen complaints involving possible criminal conduct such as various types of consumer or business related frauds, bad checks, and allegations of police misconduct. I recall investigating an allegation of date rape against a police officer that allegedly took place at the now defunct Golden Gate Motor Inn located in the Sheepshead Bay section of Brooklyn. The woman said she voluntarily went there with the officer, and they checked in using false names. She said they drank at the motel bar and became very intoxicated before going to their room where the rape allegedly happened. He then drove her home.

The police officer admitted dating the complaining witness but denied ever being at the motel or ever having forcible sexual relations with her. Back in 1971, New York law required what was known as "full corroboration" to convict on a rape charge, meaning that the testimony of a victim, even if one hundred per cent credible, had to be supported by evidence from other sources tending to establish that a sexual act took place (such as a medical examination), that physical force was used to overcome "earnest resistance" by the victim (such as evidence of physical injury or a witness who overheard screams), and that the accused was the person who committed the act (such an admission by the accused or a witness placing the accused at the scene at the time of the alleged act; DNA evidence, now commonly used to supply this type of identification evidence, had not yet come into usage by law enforcement).

As a consequence of this corroboration requirement, unless there was either an eyewitness in addition to the victim, or a confession by the accused, it usually meant that rape charges would not be brought.

The corroboration laws were enacted ostensibly to protect innocent men against being accused and convicted solely on the emotionally charged, but false, testimony of a woman. These evidentiary barriers to prosecution of sex crimes are today viewed as having been unjust and based on a bias against women and a lack of faith in the judicial system to screen out false charges.

To me, it is disturbing to recall that these laws actually existed in my own lifetime. It took many years of campaigning by women's rights groups and other concerned parties to gradually take these laws off the books which came to pass during my years as an Assistant District Attorney. The strict corroboration laws began to change in New York in the late 1970's and continued through the 1980's. It is New York's sad history that thousands of valid rape cases evaded prosecution due to these strict corroboration laws.

Nevertheless, the corroboration requirement for these cases was the law in 1971. The total absence of corroborative evidence in the case - as well as the equally credible denials by the police officer - required that the investigation be closed.

Another case I "investigated" involved a police officer on patrol who was called to the scene of an on-going store robbery. According to the police reports taken from civilian witnesses who were there as well as the statement made to investigators by the police officer, when the officer arrived, the robber had a gun pointed at the store owner and others in the store. The uniformed officer drew his gun, and shouted, "Police. Drop your gun." The robber turned towards the officer but did not drop his gun. The officer then shot the robber killing him.

My assignment was to review the evidence and determine if this apparently clearly justified shooting warranted any further action by the District Attorney's Office. Under the law, a shooting would be justified if the officer reasonably believed firing his weapon was necessary to protect his life or the life of another person. After reviewing the reports and the relevant law, I wrote a memo to the Bureau Chief recommending that the matter be closed, because I concluded the police officer's actions could not be shown to be criminal under the law.

The Bureau Chief, Edward Rappaport, was one of the two men who had initially interviewed me only a few months before and whose questions had caused me to exit the interview through the wrong door. I took extra pains to write a memo that would impress him. After I submitted the memo, he called me into his office. He said he had also read the case file and agreed with my conclusion that the shooting was justified.

However, he noted in a matter-of-fact tone that was as minimally critical of me as possible under the circumstances that I had not mentioned in my memo that the robber was found to have been holding a toy gun rather than a real one. He showed me a document, and I realized I had overlooked the one sentence in the multiple reports which stated that the robber's gun was a toy.

Because the gun looked real enough to have fooled all the people in the store, the police officer's belief that the gun posed a mortal danger to himself and others was, nevertheless, reasonable. Therefore, the conclusion that the shooting was legally justified remained correct, although my analysis was incomplete.

From my oversight in this case, I learned not only to try to be more careful when reviewing documents, but also, as a result of Mr. Rappaport's accepting my mistake without berating me, that showing patience with subordinates goes a long way to earning their respect and loyalty.

The second main function of a Criminal Law Investigator was to "ride" cases, which involved going to police stations to take stenographically recorded statements from suspects and witnesses in cases where someone was killed or "was likely to die," cases where police shot a civilian, or "publicity" cases," as they were called, involving crimes the press might write about, such as cases where a public figure was involved.

When I was in the Investigations Bureau, the way the riding program worked was that during the day more experienced Assistant District Attorneys who were assigned to the trial bureaus did the riding, and we would accompany them in order to learn how to do it. After doing this once or twice, we were deemed capable of going on our own and were primarily responsible for riding at night and secondarily responsible for riding during the day when the Assistant from the trial bureau was already out on another case.

During our night riding shift, we were on call and reached by a beeper (considered "modern technology" back then) notifying us to call the Office. On receiving the beep, we would call the Office and be told by a dispatcher which police precinct to report to. We were authorized to then call the nearest police precinct, even if it was not in Brooklyn, and be driven in a police car to the precinct where the statements were to be taken. A stenographer employed by the District Attorney's Office would be separately driven to meet us there. After speaking with the detective in charge of the case to learn what was involved, we would then take our stenographically recorded statements.

Today, these statements are, instead, electronically recorded either on audio or video which makes for a far more dramatic impression when used as evidence in a courtroom. It depicts the defendant's own voice and facial expressions as compared to a transcript read to the jury. Electronic recording also makes it more difficult for the defense to argue that evidence of the statement has been fabricated, altered, or inaccurately transcribed by the stenographer.

We were required to advise the person arrested of his *Miranda* rights, meaning the right to remain silent, a warning that anything he said could be used against him in court, that he had the right to an attorney, and that if he could not afford an attorney, one would be provided free of charge, and also ask if he understood each right, and, if so, if he wanted to answer questions. An actual recording of this procedure is better evidence in court than a cold transcript to demonstrate whether the accused was actually given these warnings, understood them, and voluntarily agreed to make a statement.

A video recording is also valuable evidence to ascertain whether the accused appears to have been well-treated by the police prior to making the statement or whether he appears to have been sleep deprived or in an agitated state which might have a bearing on the voluntariness of the accused's decision to make a statement. The initial questioning by the police, however, was not recorded, and, today, despite the urging by many criminal justice advocates to do so, in most cases this still is not done in New York.

In situations where a person arrested agreed to make a statement, it was usually because the accused either wished to deny being involved or attempted to mitigate responsibility by claiming the injury or death caused was an accident or done in self-defense. Even these so-called exculpatory statements could be valuable to the prosecution, because they would lock the accused into a version of the events that could be used at trial to challenge (the legal term is "impeach") any testimony by the accused that differed from the version given to the prosecutor in the police station.

I do not recall any particular case where I took statements other than the one where a teenager arrested for a shooting after being identified by a witness denied being involved and told us he had a twin brother who may have been the culprit. I never found out what happened to that case.

The goal of a newly hired Criminal Law Investigator was to serve as little time as possible in the Investigations Bureau and then move on to the courtroom. My time to move came in September of 1971.

Chapter 3. *THE CRIMINAL COURT BUILDING*

The District Attorney's Criminal Court Bureau was appropriately situated in what is commonly referred to as the Criminal Court Building (trivia experts know that the cornerstone actually says "Central Courts Building") located at 120 Schermerhorn Street. To appreciate what it was like to work there, the setting is an important component.

The building was constructed between 1929 and 1932. It is an eleven-story Renaissance Revival style edifice with limestone clad upper walls on a granite base. The front facade has three, three-story arched entrances set in a four-story rusticated base.

On the inside, the two-story lobby has a coffered ceiling. The lobby has two courtrooms which are used to arraign newly arrested defendants. Prior to these arraignments, attorneys are assigned to represent defendants if they cannot afford an attorney. Both courtrooms operate weekdays, and at least one of the courtrooms is also open on weekends and holidays. There is also a seven-day-a-week night court session for arraignments from 5:00 pm to 1:00 am. Family members wait in these courtrooms for their relatives' cases to be called, which can take up to 24 hours or more from the time of the arrest. In the lobby there are often attorneys discreetly approaching these family members and letting them know their services are available. One attorney, known as "The Count" would simply lean on his large Rolls Royce parked in front of the courthouse and let his bespoke wardrobe advertise his availability. Other attorneys would don an elbow-patched sport jacket, sport a pony tail, and linger in the lobby to let their potential clients know they were available "to fight the system" at a reasonable price.

There are bronze railings and bronze elevator doors in the large marble covered lobby. When working, the five elevators were usually so overcrowded that attorneys, both prosecutors and defense counsel, would feel free to use the single elevator reserved for judges which delayed and overcrowded that elevator. This, in turn, caused some judges, including myself, to either use the stairs or share an elevator located in a back hallway with handcuffed prisoners and their court officer escorts. In fact, it was on that elevator on the morning of September 11, 2001, that I first heard from a court clerk, that a plane had crashed into the World Trade Center.

The courtrooms are paneled in wood with matching wooden benches and decorative plaster ceilings. Just about every wooden bench had initials carved into them and the plaster ceilings on the top floor courtrooms were peeling due to the leaky roof that could never be properly fixed. The courtrooms were lit with large chandeliers that were hung from the extremely high ceilings. Through the glass bottoms of some chandeliers close observation would reveal paper clips and rubber bands, no doubt shot there by bored court personnel when the courtrooms were empty.

In 1992, when I was appointed an Acting Supreme Court Justice, I was assigned to a courtroom on the tenth floor of the Criminal Court building, because the Supreme Court building a few blocks away did not have enough courtrooms. I remained assigned there, except for about three years when I sat in Supreme Court on Staten Island, until 2005 when a new Supreme Court Building opened.

Because there was no central air-conditioning, large window air conditioners were used, which were so noisy they had to be turned off so juries could hear the witnesses testify. To keep the courtroom cool, the large windows were opened. On occasion, a pigeon would fly through an open window and not be able to find its way back outside. Needless to say, the building had its issues — a combination of grandeur and organized chaos.

In 1971 when I first arrived as an Assistant District Attorney, and thereafter, this courthouse was used to process the tens of thousands of annual arrests in Brooklyn, both misdemeanors and felonies. Misdemeanor cases stayed in the building until they were concluded by either a guilty plea, a dismissal, or a trial. Felony cases stayed in the building until it was decided whether that case would be indicted by a Grand Jury. If indicted, the case would be transferred to the Supreme Court located either in a much newer building a few blocks away or to courtrooms, like the one I was to have, located on the upper floors of the Criminal Court Building. In the Supreme Court, the volume of cases was far less but the stakes in terms of the potential jail time carried by the felony case were far higher.

Chapter 4. *THE TRAINING IN CRIMINAL COURT*

On my first day assigned to the Criminal Court Bureau, I was seated with several other newly hired Assistant District Attorneys in the Office of the Criminal Court Bureau Chief, David Epstein. He was tall, courtly, gray-haired, and soon to become an elected Judge of the Civil Court. He told us that we were going to be assigned with one or two other Assistants to various courtrooms and that we would be responsible for handling the 75 to 125 cases calendared each day. To distinguish one courtroom from another, each courtroom is given a number and prefaced by the word "Part," meaning that the courtroom is a "part" of the entire court.

Some Parts had cases that were just on for conferences and possible guilty pleas or dismissals. Other Parts had cases that were actually scheduled for hearings or trials. There were also "specialized" Parts, such as the Part that had only cases where the defendants were l6 but less than 19 years old, who were eligible for more lenient "youthful offender" treatment or a Part designated to handle gambling cases.

The "gambling" Part was for defendants charged with profiting from "gambling activity" involving what was known as "numbers games" which was similar to a state lottery. The winning "numbers" were determined by the digits in the totals bet at a particular race track and could be found in the daily papers. Cases for the gambling Parts were generated by arrests made by a special unit of the police department devoted to investigating and making arrests in these cases. Merely playing or betting on these numbers was not a crime. The laws targeted the operators of these betting games.

This police unit that enforced these laws was disbanded in the 1970's by the Police Department when it was decided that the risks of police corruption and bribery from the operators of these gambling enterprises surpassed the law enforcement benefits that might result from devoting police resources to making arrests in these cases. This was a central theme of the award-winning, Brooklyn-based movie "Serpico," starring Al Pacino in the title role.

Indeed, I recall one case I handled involving a defendant who was arrested after he "dropped" gambling slips on the street when the police officer approached him. The police officer, after speaking with the defendant's attorney in the hallway prior to testifying, admitted that he "lost sight" of the slips after the defendant dropped them. This testimony created a doubt in the mind of the judge hearing the case that the papers the officer picked up were the same papers he saw the defendant drop. It seemed everyone involved in the case, except me, knew what really was going on.

New Assistants were told that we were to be guided by the more experienced Assistant District Attorney assigned to the Part with us. At the time, each Bureau in the Office had a Chief and a Deputy Chief, but they generally did not go into the courtrooms to observe and be immediately available to answer questions. There was no intermediate level of supervision by someone who was assigned to train new Assistants and who would be responsible for directly overseeing their work on a daily basis.

In the Criminal Court, the Assistant in the Part with the most experience was the person who was supposed to train the newcomer, even if the experience differential was a matter of weeks. Sometimes the senior person in the Part was either a chronic underachiever and was not being promoted out of Criminal Court or someone who had been "returned to Criminal Court" after a poor evaluation in his new assignment. Thus, careless work habits and misinformation about the law could easily be passed to new Assistants, which all too often occurred.

As far as the Office's policies regarding what cases to plea bargain, meaning in what situations an Assistant was authorized to recommend a guilty plea to a lesser charge or recommend less than the maximum sentence, we were told that the District Attorney hired us because he trusted our discretion. There were no written policies or guidelines. As long as we had the case file and looked at it before taking the guilty plea and, if called upon, could give a reason for doing what we did, the Office would support our decision. This turned out to be true in practice, and it gave most of us a strong sense of loyalty to the Office knowing that our plea bargaining decisions would be supported even if criticized by the victim, the press, or the police officers involved in the case.

We were not required to consult with the victim before deciding whether to accept a guilty plea to a lesser charge or even inform the victim of the outcome of the case. This callous practice has long-since been abandoned.

There were two informal guidelines as passed down to us by the more senior Criminal Court Assistants: First, was the "20-stitch rule" which meant that a felony assault charge could be reduced to a misdemeanor assault if the injuries required less than 20 stitches. The second was the "10-ounce rule" which meant that a felony charge of marijuana possession could be reduced to a misdemeanor if the case involved possession of less than 10 ounces.

It should be noted that back in 1971, by statute, the Criminal Court did not have jurisdiction over "domestic violence" cases, which included misdemeanor assaults between spouses or members of the same household. These were matters the law reserved for resolution in the Family Court in a civil rather than a criminal proceeding.

In the 1980's, the law was legislatively changed, giving both the Criminal and Family Courts concurrent jurisdiction over these cases and specifying that the victim had the choice in which court to proceed. Subsequently, the choice given to the victim was also legislatively eliminated, and the District Attorney's Office was given the exclusive right to determine whether to prosecute these cases criminally or allow the matter to be resolved in Family Court.

Alternative forms of sentencing such as community service, restitution, and many types of drug and alcohol treatment programs that now are commonly part of sentences in misdemeanor cases were rarely, if ever, employed. With fewer sentencing options available, there were fewer things for a prosecutor to consider when making a plea offer.

Years later when I sat as a Criminal Court Judge in Brooklyn, the Assistant District Attorneys had a list of plea bargaining rules and corresponding sentencing options depending of the type of case and the defendant's criminal record, if any. These rules minutely controlled the plea offers that could be made, sometimes requiring the approval of a supervisor to change the recommended fine from $100 to $50, or the number of days of community service from three days to two.

At times, because of the lack of discretion now given to Assistants actually handling a case in Criminal Court, some Assistants seemed almost robotic in reciting the Office's plea bargaining position in a case. Whether the Assistant personally believed the plea offer being made was appropriate, or even whether the Assistant had actually given the question any thought, was irrelevant. As a result, among other things, it seemed to me that new Assistants did not have to call upon their judgment and discretion as much as their earlier counterparts. Whether this was a good or bad development in the overall administration of justice is certainly a debatable question.

Strict plea bargaining guidelines promote consistency in plea offers regardless of which Assistant is handling the case and are designed to reflect the "office policy" as approved by the District Attorney. The judgment of a more seasoned prosecutor is also more likely to reflect a more intelligent evaluation of the strengths and weakness of the case as well as better serve the interests of the victim and protect the Office from the consequences a gross mistake by a new Assistant. These are all good things.

On the other hand, no two cases are exactly alike and deviations from the guidelines, whether upwards or downwards, should always be considered. Where the Assistant in the courtroom does not have the sole authority to make that decision, this results in the case being adjourned for a supervisor to review the Office's plea position. This causes delay in the case and adds additional cases to the calendar the next day that case in on, meaning that the parties to the other cases on the calendar that day spend more time in the courtroom waiting for their respective case to be called. There is also an additional expense to the public resulting from the delay if the defendant is indigent and the defendant's court-appointed attorney is being paid by the hour at public expense.

What has not thus far been taken into account in this discussion, is that any plea offer by a prosecutor must be approved by the judge handling the case who ultimately has the responsibility for approving the plea and sentence imposed. As a Criminal Court Judge, it was frustrating not to be able to dispose of a misdemeanor case with a plea and sentence that I believed was appropriate, if the Assistant in the Part did not have the authority to do so based on "office policy," even if the disagreement was over only a matter of a few dollars in the fine or a day or two of community service in the sentence.

Chapter 5. *IN THE COURTROOMS OF THE CRIMINAL COURT*

Because I was assigned to Criminal Court for only about three months, I do not have many specific memories of my courtroom experiences. We were generally assigned to a particular court Part and judge for about a week at a time. Because the schedules of Assistants assigned to Criminal Court called for their rotations to other assignments in the Office, Assistants had to be constantly moved from Part to Part. However, the cases stayed in the Part, and so it was rare for an Assistant in Criminal Court to see a case more than once. Assistants had to learn how to pick up a case file in court when the case was called by the clerk, quickly scan it to see what it was about, and then be prepared to make whatever decisions about the case that were required.

I don't recall having to do any paperwork on any case. In fact, I don't even recall having a desk of my own. The District Attorney's Office had the use of a corner of the building on one of the middle floors for office use by the Criminal Court Bureau. Assistants were assigned cubby hole locker space to hold personal items in a large room with several desks and telephones to be shared with other Assistants.

During my first week in a courtroom, I picked up a file concerning a young man charged with felony possession of a loaded gun. When the case was called into the record, the defense attorney asked the court for a "second call" so he could speak to me about a plea offer. As with all felony cases in Criminal Court, this case was pending either a transfer to the Supreme Court after an indictment by a Grand Jury or a reduction of the charge to a misdemeanor after which there could then be either a trial or a guilty plea.

The defendant had been interviewed prior to arraignment by a City agency for the purpose of assisting the court in its determination of whether to set bail or release the defendant without bail. The report of that interview in the file indicated that the defendant was a full-time high school student and lived with his parents. His fingerprint report showed this was his first arrest. In the absence of any indication that the defendant had an intent to use the gun unlawfully, and probably also based on the factual account the defense attorney gave me - which I don't recall - of how the defendant came to be in possession of that gun, I drew upon my "discretion" and determined that the charge should be reduced to a misdemeanor. Years later, a change in the Criminal Procedure Law statute controlling when a felony case pending in Criminal Court involving a gun could be reduced to a misdemeanor would have prohibited what I determined was the right thing to do in this case.

Based on the defendant's age and lack of prior criminal record, a misdemeanor plea would likely result in Youthful Offender treatment by the court and no public criminal record of the conviction.

Before agreeing with the defense attorney to reduce the charge, I noticed the Bureau Chief, Mr. Epstein, leaning against the wall near the front of the crowded courtroom. I decided to show him that I was not some reckless new Assistant District Attorney who would not take advantage of an opportunity to have a far more experienced prosecutor review the decision I had just made. I walked over to Mr. Epstein and re-introduced myself as a newly assigned Assistant District Attorney. I then quickly told him the pertinent facts and asked him if he thought I should reduce the charge. When he responded, "Sounds good to me," my confidence in my judgment received a terrific boost.

Shortly after, the case was called again. The court approved the reduction of the charges. The defendant pled guilty to a misdemeanor, and the case was adjourned for the sentence that did not involve any time in jail for the defendant.

When the next case was called, "Mr. Epstein" who had approved the guilty plea stood before the court and announced that he was "Murray Cutler" appearing as the defense attorney in that case. He did bear some resemblance to my Bureau Chief, but I realized I had made a very embarrassing mistake: I had obtained "approval" to reduce the felony charge from a defense attorney rather than my Bureau Chief.

I guess Murray Cutler must have been flattered and surprised that a young Assistant District Attorney would seek his opinion, and he did not realize I thought he was Mr. Epstein. In any event, the right result, in my opinion, was achieved, and I was relieved my mistake slipped under the Mr. Epstein's radar.

Years later, Murray Cutler's son, Bruce Cutler, became an Assistant District Attorney in Brooklyn and a colleague of mine. After leaving the Office, Bruce became a defense attorney and gained national recognition with his successful courtroom representation of organized crime family leader John Gotti. But I doubt that as a defense attorney he ever equaled his father's achievement of approving a prosecutor's plea offer in a case he had nothing to do with.

The Judges of the Criminal Court are appointed by the Mayor for 10-year terms. It was not uncommon for Mayors to dispense these appointments as political rewards, a situation that changed in the 1980's when Mayor Koch instituted a non-partisan committee of attorneys to screen all candidates for his judicial appointments.

Until that time, the Criminal Court bench was heavily populated with former State and City legislators and other political types who were capping their careers with a judicial appointment. What these judges may have lacked in experience in criminal law, they more than made up for in life experience and engaging, although sometimes eccentric, personalities.

During a break in court proceedings one morning, a judge fitting the profile I just described was chatting with myself and the Legal Aid Society attorney who was also assigned to the Part that week. The judge told us a joke involving a shoplifter in a variety store who put some items in his pocket and then went to the cashier with the intent of paying for just one small item. The cashier rang up the shoplifter's small item and then said, "For the pens in your right pocket, that will be $4.00 and for the candy in your left pocket, that will be $6.00." The judge continued the joke, saying that the shoplifter was so shocked at being caught that he farted, causing the clerk to say, "And for the duck call in your back pocket that will be $7.00."

Well, although I politely laughed, as a recent law school graduate and as someone who until a few weeks before had never even spoken to a judge, I could never imagine a judge actually telling a joke with a fart as a punchline. Perhaps it was at that moment that I knew that I too could someday be a judge.

I also recall being assigned to Night Court arraignments for a week in September of 1971. The shift began an 5:00 pm and ran until about 1:00 am. There were no other Assistant District Attorneys in the building, and I was a new and on my own. The case would be called, I was supposed to quickly read the file and make a brief statement about the case and the defendant's prior criminal record, if any, to the judge and then either ask that bail be set in a specific amount based on the seriousness of the charges or consent that the defendant be released without bail. The defense attorney would then be heard on the question of bail, and the judge would then make a bail decision.

For someone with as little courtroom experience as I had at the time and no experience at all doing this type of proceeding, it was quite a learning experience, but doing about 75 cases a night and being told by the judge in open court when he disagreed with my recommendations enabled me to gain some idea how to do it, or at least get by.

What made that week even more memorable, if not also tension filled, was that it coincided with the infamous Attica prison riot where corrections officers were being held hostage for several days. Ultimately, negotiations failed and the takeover was forcibly ended in a law enforcement raid resulting in the deaths of dozens of hostages and prisoners. The atmosphere in the courtroom every night seemed especially tense as the Attica tragedy unfolded, and I was asking that bail be set in case after case. I felt as if the stares from the defendants' family members in the audience were also blaming me for the Attica events. When combined with my anxiety in carrying out this arraignment assignment for the first time, the awful events of Attica magnified my discomfort.

Chapter 6. *THE APPEALS BUREAU - THE START*

After spending about three months in various assignments in the Criminal Court Bureau, the new Bureau Chief who had replaced Mr. Epstein told me I was being transferred to the Appeals Bureau. I had not asked for this transfer and no one ever discussed it with me. I was planning on the "normal" rotation of about one year in the Criminal Court Bureau, one year in the Grand Jury Bureau learning how to present felony cases to a Grand Jury, and then a transfer to the Supreme Court Bureau for felony trial experience.

The Appeals Bureau was generally reserved for those regarded by some as "eggheads" who specifically requested that assignment. I don't know if my transfer there was planned from the time I was hired based on the excellent reputations of the college (Brown) and the law school (New York University) I attended or on my performance in the Criminal Court Bureau. If the latter, I hope it was not because my supervisors believed I had no future as a trial lawyer.

Anyway, the transfer to Appeals turned out to be a significant turning point in my legal career. Not only did I learn writing and legal research skills that would be invaluable for the rest of my legal career, I also began to develop a reputation in the Office as a go to person who could give quick answers to legal questions from Assistants calling from the courtrooms where they were on trial. Some of these questions were a little tricky, but most involved straightforward issues that could be answered by someone who had spent a minimal amount of time reading appellate decisions in a law library or who had a basic familiarity with the statutes contained in the then newly-enacted Criminal Procedure Law which went into effect in September of 1971.

There were four other first-year Assistants like myself assigned to the Bureau, two of whom, Richard Carruthers and Alan Marrus, like myself, eventually became Criminal Court and, subsequently, Acting Supreme Court Judges. The Appeals Bureau attorneys in the class hired the year before were also excellent lawyers whose guidance to me was both generous and invaluable. Together with the Deputy Chief of the Appeals Bureau, Helman Brook, a brilliant lawyer just a few years older than myself and among the first non-political hires of District Attorney Gold, as well as my office-mate, Roger Adler, hired the year before me, the young lawyers I worked with in the Appeals Bureau were truly outstanding.

There was a considerable gap in experience between that second-year group and the next group of five attorneys who were all in their 60's and who had all been in the Office for many years. They were dedicated, seasoned attorneys and provided role models of courtesy and professionalism.

The Chief of the Bureau, William I. Siegel, was also in his 60's and was renowned, not only in Brooklyn judicial circles, but throughout the State for his scholarship and integrity. He personally argued several cases before the United States Supreme Court which established important legal precedents in the areas of confessions and search and seizure.

"Mr. Siegel" as we all fondly called him, was known in appellate courts for his willingness, where appropriate, to "confess error" and concede that a conviction should be reversed rather than put forth a legal argument which he did not believe had merit. He understood that the true role of a prosecutor was to seek justice. His own actions exemplified an ethical standard that it was an honor to attempt to emulate.

His reputation for integrity and candor literally preceded him as illustrated by what happened when I was dispatched to a Supreme Court Judge's chambers to help another Assistant argue a legal point involving a trial of a perjury case.

The defendant in that perjury case was on trial for having falsely testified as an alibi witness for his friend who had been charged with a murder in Brooklyn. The alibi for the person charged with murder was that he was in a hospital in Puerto Rico at the time of the murder. The alibi was presented by the defendant at the later perjury trial who testified he visited his friend in that hospital at the time of the murder.

After his friend was acquitted in the murder trial, an investigation of the hospital's records (which was not done before the murder trial) revealed that the defendant charged with murder, in fact, was not a patient in that hospital at the time of the murder. Based on these records, the alibi witness was charged with committing perjury at his friend's murder trial for testifying that he visited his friend in the hospital at a time when the records showed the friend was not there.

The legal issue that now concerned the judge trying the perjury case was that under New York's perjury statute, a person could not be convicted of perjury "on the testimony of a single witness." The trial judge was considering the defense attorney's argument that the hospital records tending to show the alleged alibi was false was the equivalent of "a single witness." I argued that documents were not the equivalent of "a witness," but the judge said, "I want to hear what Mr. Siegel has to say." I called Mr. Siegel and explained the situation. He came to the judge's chambers to make the same argument I had just made.

When Mr. Siegel entered the room, the Judge, William Cowan, who had a reputation as being somewhat "colorful," got up from behind his desk and said, "Mr. Siegel, thank you for coming over. Let me kiss your ring." The judge then approached Mr. Siegel and, to everyone's astonishment, took Mr. Siegel's hand and kissed it. I saw the defense attorney slump in his chair. Needless to say, the exact argument I had unsuccessfully made prevailed after it was repeated to Judge Cowan by Mr. Siegel.

The District Attorney's Office has constructed a moot courtroom where Assistants can practice their skills. That courtroom is named in honor of Mr. Siegel who left the Office before most of the people now using that courtroom were born. I was privileged to have worked with him.

Chapter 7. *THE APPEALS BUREAU - LEARNING THE ROPES*

In my year-and-a-half in the Appeals Bureau, I had the opportunity to develop a wide range of litigation skills that would be put to good use for the next 45 years of my legal career.

I learned how to write appellate briefs and argue in appellate courts. The initial assignments involved straightforward issues in felony cases of lesser seriousness such as whether the sentence imposed was unduly excessive. My first appeal of this kind involved a man who had stabbed his two infant children to death in their crib. He pleaded guilty to two counts of Manslaughter and received a sentences, as I recall, totaling about 45 years in prison. The photographs of the children's bloody bodies in their crib that were in the case file were more convincing than anything I could have written to justify that sentence.

In another case, I wrote an appellate brief responding to a claim by the defendant on appeal that the trial court should have declared a mistrial when the prosecutor made an improper comment in front of the jury which the defendant argued deprived him of a fair trial. Unfortunately, I do not recall the nature of the comment, but the comment itself is not what makes this case memorable to me.

I argued in my brief that the prosecutor's comment did not warrant declaring a mistrial, and, in any event, the defendant's trial attorney did not even request a mistrial. Instead, the defendant's attorney asked for "withdrawal of a juror." I had never heard of that expression, and I did not bother to try to find out what it meant before submitting my brief to the Appellate Division, which is the New York Court that hears appeals taken from the New York Supreme Court.

The day before that case was scheduled for oral argument, I decided to research the meaning of the expression "withdrawal of a juror." I learned to my shock that it was derived from an English common law practice in civil cases to end a jury trial before its conclusion where the circumstances warranted by means of the court ordering that one of the jurors leave the jury box. Thus, the argument I had made in my brief that the defendant did not ask for a mistrial was not correct, although the request was phrased in rather arcane terminology. It was too late to file an amended brief.

When appearing before the Appellate Division the next day, I began my oral argument by apologizing for arguing in my brief that defendant did not ask for a mistrial and that I had only learned the day before that asking for "withdrawal of a juror" was, in effect, asking for a mistrial. The Presiding Judge, J. Irwin Shapiro, an extremely astute jurist who was notorious for giving unprepared lawyers a hard time, simply smiled, gave me a dismissive wave of his hand, and said, "Yes. We know. Go on with your argument."

Despite my embarrassing misstep, the Appellate Division affirmed the conviction based on my argument that the trial court was correct in not declaring a mistrial, because the prosecutor's conduct was not so egregious as to deny the defendant a fair trial. As for not doing the research on the meaning of "withdrawal of a juror" until after I had submitted my brief, that was a lesson I tried not to forget.

Another appellate case I had involved Francois Scaglia, who was one of several defendants convicted after a trial of conspiring to sell over a 100 pounds of heroin with a street value of about 50 million dollars. This case resulted in a book and an Academy Award winning movie, both titled "The French Connection." In the movie, Scaglia, a native of Corsica, was the character who hijacked an elevated subway in Brooklyn and was thrillingly chased in a car below by Detective Eddie Egan, played by Gene Hackman, who eventually caught up to Scaglia on the train and shot him. That aspect of the movie never happened. Although the movie was largely factual, there was no subway chase and Scaglia was never shot.

In the 1960's, Scaglia was tried, convicted, and sentenced to prison. He appealed, and the conviction was affirmed. The book and the movie followed. In fact, the book was dedicated to Frank Bauman, the Assistant District Attorney who tried the case. I became involved in 1972, shortly after the movie was released. Scaglia's attorney had filed motion to vacate the conviction on several grounds that were not raised on his prior appeal. That motion was denied by a Judge of the Supreme Court who decided the motion in place of the original trial judge who had retired.

Among the issues raised in Scalia's appeal from the denial of the motion, was that during the trial in Brooklyn Supreme Court, Scaglia's attorney told the trial judge that he could not return for the afternoon session, because he had to appear on another case in County Court. The trial judge, the Hon. Samuel Leibowitz, famous in his own right for many things including his defense in the 1930's of the "Scottsboro Boys" — a notorious case in Alabama where several black men were accused of raping a white woman — noted that the County Court in New York City no longer existed, having been merged in New York City several years before into the State Supreme Court.

Believing that Scalia's lawyer may have become mentally disoriented, or perhaps just wanting to "protect the record" against a claim that the lawyer had become mentally incompetent, Judge

Leibowitz ordered that the lawyer undergo a mental examination by a court appointed psychiatrist.

The examination was completed that same day. The psychiatrist determined that the lawyer was fatigued from the trial and, although momentarily confused, was, nevertheless, fit to continue with the trial. The trial then resumed and Scaglia was thereafter convicted.

In the appeal that I handled, Scaglia argued that at the time his lawyer was being examined by the psychiatrist, Scaglia should have had another lawyer representing him, because Scaglia's lawyer had a conflict of interest between his duty to Scaglia to admit that he was too disoriented to continue, if that was in fact true, and his financial self-interest in not being found mentally unfit to continue. My response, in part, was that the Appellate Division should not consider this argument at this stage of the proceedings, because there were sufficient facts on the record at the time of the defendant's first appeal for this argument to have been made at that time. The Appellate Division upheld Scaglia's conviction without writing a decision.

There are two footnotes to this anecdote. First, is that at the time I was working on this appeal, the 50 million dollars' worth of heroin involved in the case was found to have been stolen from the Police Department Property Clerk's warehouse. Eventually, this theft was linked to members of a special narcotics unit of the police department that became the subject of yet another movie, "Prince of the City."

Thus, if Scaglia's conviction had been reversed and a new trial ordered, the heroin that was the subject of that trial would not have been available to be introduced in evidence, a prospect that the District Attorney personally discussed with me as I was working on the case.

A more pleasant footnote concerns a charitable fundraising showing of "The French Connection" at Lincoln Center that I attended about 40 years later. As part of the program, after the movie was shown, retired Detective Sonny Grosso, who was involved in the actual French Connection case and portrayed in the movie by Roy Scheider, answered questions from the audience. Prior to the screening, I had the opportunity to introduce myself to Detective Grosso and told him that before I was a judge, I worked on the case as an Assistant District Attorney. I showed him a copy of the Scaglia brief I had brought with me and asked him to autograph it for me. He kindly agreed. Above his signature, he wrote, "Please don't sell this." We both laughed.

In addition to brief writing responsibilities, first-year Assistants in the Appeals Bureau had the assignment of responding in Part One of the Supreme Court to all written motions made in pending felony cases. Under the then-existing court rules, even though pending felony cases were assigned to various judges assigned to the Criminal Term of the Supreme Court, if a defendant wished to make a written motion in that case, these motions had to be made before a different judge in Part One.

These motions were mostly routine and made in every case, such as a request for an order directing the prosecutor to provide further information about the case or a request that the court read the Grand Jury minutes to insure that the charges were based on legally sufficient evidence and that the Grand Jury presentation was fair and in accordance with the law. Sometimes the motions were not so routine and were dependent of the facts of the particular case and less well-known statutes and legal principles.

The reason for relieving the judge assigned to the case from the task of deciding written motions on that case was never explained to me. Perhaps it was to done to allow the judge assigned to the case more time to spend on actual trials and place the burden of handling the paperwork involved in reading motions and writing decisions on one judge at a time.

The judicial assignment to Part One was rotated every four weeks and was limited to about five of the most experienced and knowledgeable judges of the approximately 20 judges then assigned to the Supreme Court. As some of these judges retired or were elevated to the Appellate Division of the Supreme Court, other talented judges took their place in the Part One rotation.

The reason why the Assistant District Attorneys who were assigned to try these cases were not also responsible for answering these motions in Part One was never explained to me. For whatever reason, even though the cases were assigned to Assistant District Attorneys who were not assigned to the Appeals Bureau for purposes of trying those cases, an Appeals Bureau Assistant District Attorney was assigned to handle these motions before a judge who also was not assigned to the case.

The five first-year Assistants in the Appeals Bureau rotated on a weekly basis before the experienced judge handling these Part One motions. We were each responsible for answering every motion that was before the Court for that week. This gave us the invaluable opportunity to have experience in the Supreme Court in felony cases at least two years before our peers and learn not only the basic procedural law involving these cases, but also the less commonly encountered legal principles that were the subjects of some of these motions. We also had the opportunity to appear before the most experienced and knowledgeable judges of the

Supreme Court and to learn their points of view as to what facts would control their decisions.

Thus, the Appeals Bureau assignment to Part One in proved to be just as valuable a learning experience as briefing and arguing appeals.

A few years after I left the Appeals Bureau, the court rules were changed, and Part One's function as the place for all motions to be made was ended. Thereafter, motions were to be decided by the judge handling the case and, unless the motion was on a difficult issue, the Assistant assigned to the case was responsible for responding to the motion. This change resulted in more efficient case handling, but on a personal level I was, nevertheless, fortunate to have benefitted from the "inefficient" Part One procedures.

Chapter 8. *IN THE COURT OF APPEALS*

The New York court system has two levels of appeals courts for felony cases. The first level is the Appellate Division of the Supreme Court which consists of four separate courts, each responsible for a geographic area in the State called a "Department." Brooklyn is in the Second Department.

Every defendant convicted of a felony is entitled to appeal the conviction to the Appellate Division. The losing side on that appeal, whether it is the defendant or the prosecution, has the opportunity to take a further appeal to the Court of Appeals which has seven Judges and sits in Albany.

In a criminal case there is no automatic right to appeal from the Appellate Division to the Court of Appeals. Permission to appeal, called "leave to appeal," must be granted by either a judge who took part of the decision in the Appellate Division or by a judge of the Court of Appeals. Leave to appeal to the Court of Appeals in criminal cases is generally granted only where there is a significant legal issue to be decided. As a result, it is both a rare and challenging opportunity for a lawyer to argue a case before the seven judges of the Court of Appeals.

THE "RIGHT TO A PUBLIC TRIAL" IS NOT ABSOLUTE

The Rudolph Smallwood Case

My first opportunity to argue in the Court of Appeals came by a stroke of good fortune when after only a few months in the Appeals Bureau, the Bureau Chief, Mr. Siegel, called me into his office and told me he was assigning me a case where leave to appeal had already been granted but the senior Assistant District Attorney who had handled that case in the Appellate Division had retired. I would be responsible for writing the brief to the Court of Appeals and then arguing the case.

The defendant in that case had been charged with murder as the result of a shooting. He was convicted of manslaughter because his intent to cause the death of the victim had not been proven beyond a reasonable doubt. The main legal issue in the case was a claim that the defendant was deprived of his Sixth Amendment Constitutional right to a public trial when the trial court granted, over defense counsel's objection, the prosecutor's request to exclude from the courtroom the six spectators who were then present during the testimony of a 16-year-old eyewitness to the shooting who was four months' pregnant.

The prosecutor had argued that the defendant's friends were among the spectators, that the witness, although she had not been threatened, was reluctant to testify with them present. Also, the prosecutor added that the witness's mother did not want her daughter to testify, because she was afraid her daughter would "lose the baby."

On appeal, the defendant argued, among other things, that the trial judge should not have granted the request to clear the courtroom of spectators based solely on the prosecutor's assertions and should have first held a hearing out of the presence of the jury to inquire directly of the witness as to how she felt about testifying with spectators present. It was my argument that the law did not require such a hearing and that, in any event, although the defendant's lawyer at trial objected to clearing the courtroom, the lawyer did not suggest to the trial judge that the witness be personally questioned about why she was afraid to testify and whether she, in fact, would refuse to testify with spectators present.

The case was argued in the Court of Appeals in October of 1972. I had barely one year of experience in the Appeals Bureau. I drove to Albany to argue the case accompanied by my wife for moral support. The Chief Judge at the time, with three other judges sitting on each side of him, was the nationally renowned Stanley H. Fuld, whose decisions were in the law school textbooks I had studied only a few years before. Seated to Judge Fund's immediate right was Judge Charles J. Breitel, a brilliant jurist who would succeed Judge Fuld as Chief Judge. Surrounding everyone in the heavily paneled, high ceilinged courtroom were dozens of hanging portraits of former Court of Appeals judges all sternly looking down on the proceedings.

There were two or three other cases argued prior to my case. My wife and I sat in the spectator section observing as the lawyers made their arguments and answered the questions posed by the judges. Skilled appellate lawyers not only expect questions, they are able to anticipate what questions will be asked and seamlessly weave their pre-planned arguments into their answers.

Judge Breitel, in particular, sharply questioned all the lawyers in each case, homing in on the weak points of their arguments while the other judges seemed very passive by comparison. After one of Judge Breitel's pointed questions to an attorney, my wife turned and whispered to me referring to Judge Breitel, "That guy is really tough."

After about an hour of watching the other cases being argued, my case was called. I and the appellate attorney for the defendant each took our respective positions at the counsel tables. The defendant's attorney, representing the party taking the appeal, argued first. I do not recall being surprised or unprepared to answer anything that he said.

The defendant, being incarcerated and serving his sentence was not present. Although a defendant has a right to be present at the trial, an incarcerated defendant has no right to be present when the conviction is appealed, even, ironically, when the issue on appeal is the defendant's right to have the public present at his trial.

When it was my turn, I stood up prepared with my well-rehearsed traditional opening line, "May it please the Court." Before I could even begin the next sentence, Judge Breitel asked me a question about the case. And then another. And then another. In total, he asked seven consecutive questions and never gave me the opportunity to complete the first sentence I had planned to say. To top it off, after receiving my response to his seventh question, he then abruptly got up from his high backed seat, turned to the door behind the bench through which all the judges had entered, and without so much as an "excuse me," left the courtroom.

I was now facing six judges having said almost everything I had planned to say although not in the order I had planned. If I were more experienced, I am sure I would have handled the situation differently, but all I could do was pretend that what had just occurred did not happen. I returned to the first sentence I had practiced, and again said, "May it please the Court."

I do not remember what else I said during the argument, but about a month later the court affirmed the defendant's conviction without writing a formal opinion, a not uncommon practice at that time.

Although this conviction was affirmed, the law in this area has evolved. Not long after this case was decided, it was recognized that it would violate a defendant's right to a public trial to clear a courtroom of spectators in a criminal case based solely on a

42

prosecutor's statements that a particular witness is fearful and does not wish to testify in public. The trial judge would be required to take testimony from the witness or someone else with personal knowledge of the relevant facts and limit the exclusion of spectators to the minimum necessary to enable the witness to safely testify.

In fact, flashing forward to 1999, I presided at a murder trial of a defendant named Nathaniel James who allegedly shot the victim in the hallway of a Coney Island housing project. During the trial, a rather menacing looking spectator dressed in red, a well-known color worn by the Blood's gang, appeared in the audience. While he was seated there, two witnesses to the shooting who had previously described the shooter, testified they did not recall what the shooter looked like. After that testimony, the prosecutor reported that the father of the deceased told the prosecutor that he had heard from a third person that this spectator had intimidated these witnesses.

On hearing this information, as the trial judge I gave the spectator a choice of either identifying himself or leaving the courtroom. The defense attorney objected. The spectator refused to identify himself. I ordered the individual to leave the courtroom and also the floor of the courthouse where the courtroom was located, because there were other witnesses outside waiting to testify.

These other witnesses testified, and the defendant was convicted. However, on appeal the Appellate Division reversed that conviction based on my excluding the spectator, stating that the prosecutor's assertions that the spectator had harassed witnesses in the case was not a sufficient basis for the exclusion.

On that appeal, the District Attorney's Office, in its brief, cited the Smallwood case I had argued over 25 years before in the Court of Appeals where the exclusion of all spectators based on the prosecutor's assertions did not require a reversal. Nevertheless, the conviction in the James case was reversed even though the trial attorney, as did the trial attorney in the Smallwood case, did not suggest that I hold a hearing to take testimony concerning the need to exclude the public. Had I lost the Smallwood case I had argued in 1972, perhaps my ruling in 1999 would have been different.

A TRIPLE MURDER THAT WAS ALMOST A QUADRUPLE

The George Lewis Case

In 1975, I returned to the Court of Appeals with a triple murder case that I had successfully briefed and argued in the Appellate Division. Although I was no longer in the Appeals Bureau, I stayed with the case after the Court of Appeals decided to hear the defendant's appeal from the Appellate Division.

The defendant had been convicted of shooting three men whose bodies were found in three different Brooklyn police precincts on the same morning: one body in a vacant lot; one body on a staircase in an abandoned building; and one body in an alley. They all had been shot once in the head. The men all had no money on them. There were no witnesses to any of these shootings.

Later that same day, a woman, whose last name was Johnson and who also had been shot in the head, but in Manhattan not Brooklyn, woke up in a hospital bed. She told the police that she had been the girlfriend of one of the three Brooklyn victims, and the night before she had been in Brooklyn with her boyfriend and the two other Brooklyn victims as well as with the defendant and his girlfriend, named Robinson. This was the first time she had met the defendant and Robinson.

According to Johnson, the defendant had previously told the group that he had a robbery scheme where he and the three men would pretend to be drug buyers and that he had contacted drug sellers to buy drugs from them. The defendant told the three men that the plan was to rob the drug sellers of the drugs they would bring to the purported drug deal.

According to the Johnson, the defendant told the three men that they needed to bring their money "to flash" to the drug sellers and that he would take them to the sellers one at a time "so that they would not get suspicious." The defendant said that the plan was to rob the sellers of their drugs after all four arrived. However, the real plan that the defendant had mind was to kill the three men, one at a time, and take the money they each would bring with them that night.

The group met in the defendant's Brooklyn apartment. Johnson said her boyfriend asked her to accompany him to the apartment and that the defendant did not know she would be part of the group that night.

The defendant then left the apartment with one of the men. Sometime later, the defendant returned and left with the second man. And then the defendant returned and left with the third, leaving Johnson and the defendant's girlfriend, Robinson, in the apartment.

Again, after a period of time, the defendant returned alone. He told Johnson that the three men were "tied up" with the drug sellers and that he would drive Johnson back to Manhattan where she lived. On the way, while on the West Side of Manhattan very late at night, the defendant said he believed he may have a flat tire. He asked Johnson to step out of the car with him to look at it. The last thing Johnson remembered before waking up in the hospital with a gunshot wound to her head was getting out of the car and bending over to look at the defendant's tire.

The defendant was convicted after a jury trial based on the testimony of Johnson and Robinson. Robinson testified she had no prior knowledge of any plan by the defendant to kill the three men and to also shoot Johnson when he drove her home.

Although all four shootings took place in New York City, because the shooting of Johnson took place in Manhattan, which under State law is a separate county and legal jurisdiction from Brooklyn, the defendant could not be charged and prosecuted in Brooklyn for the Manhattan crimes of attempted murder and assault against Johnson. He received three life sentences for the three Brooklyn murders. He was not charged in Manhattan with the Johnson shooting that took place there.

The main issue on appeal was the decision by the trial judge to allow Johnson to testify about the shooting in Manhattan even though the defendant was not charged with that crime. In order to protect a defendant from being convicted based on evidence of his generally bad character or criminal propensities rather than on actual proof that he committed the crimes charged, there is a legal restriction concerning when a prosecutor may introduce evidence of uncharged crimes. Relying on this legal principal, the defendant argued that the evidence that the defendant also shot Johnson that night was unduly prejudicial and should not have been heard by the jury.

At the time of this appeal, there were several well-known exceptions to the general restriction against introducing evidence of uncharged crimes, such as: when the uncharged crime would tend to establish the defendant's motive to commit the crime charged; when the uncharged crime would tend to establish the defendant's identity as the person who committed the crime charged; when the uncharged crime would tend to establish the absence of an otherwise innocent mistake by the defendant in committing the crime charged; when the uncharged crime would tend to show the intent of the defendant to commit the crime charged, or when the uncharged crime, along with the crime charged, were parts of a single common scheme or plan.

From a legal point of view, the shooting of Johnson in Manhattan seemed to fit one or more of these exceptions. In particular, the defendant's shooting Johnson tended to establish both his identity as the shooter of the other three men as well as his intent to kill the other three men.

Another exception, not widely recognized in appellate precedent at the time of this trial, but commonly recognized today, would be when the evidence of the uncharged crime is necessary "to complete the narrative." In this case, Johnson's account of what happened that night would be far less believable to a trial jury if the defendant had taken no measures to insure that Johnson would not be alive to tell the police that her boyfriend and his two companions had all been with the defendant that night but never came back to the defendant's apartment with him. Therefore, to "complete her narrative" of the events, it would be necessary for Johnson to testify that the defendant also tried to kill her that night.

As for the defendant also not taking measures to also eliminate his own girlfriend Robinson as a potential witness, as the evidence revealed at trial, the defendant could trust Robinson not to go to the police. When the police went to speak with Robinson after hearing what Johnson had to say after she woke up in the hospital, Robinson at first denied knowing anything about what happened to the three dead men. But after the police told Robinson that Johnson was alive after being shot by the defendant, Robinson suddenly remembered everything that she had seen and heard that night, although she denied knowing in advance that the defendant had planned to shoot the three men and Johnson.

Robinson told the police that she only learned what had happened after the defendant returned to the apartment and told her he had shot and killed "all four of them." Still, Robinson did not go to the police with this information but, instead, only revealed it after learning Johnson was alive and obviously now could implicate her in the defendant's murder plans.

This case actually seemed pretty clear cut, and I did not expect that leave to appeal would be granted to the defendant to appeal to the Court of Appeals. What I did not take into account was that the defendant's appellate attorney, Richard Farrell, who was a Professor of Evidence at Brooklyn Law School and a true expert in this legal field, had previously been a law clerk a former judge on the Court of Appeals.

The process for obtaining leave to appeal in this case involved the court assigning the leave application to one of the court's seven judges, all of whom had chambers in their home towns as well as in Albany. This case was assigned to a judge who had chambers in Queens. The procedure was to go to the judge's chambers for "a leave hearing."

I appeared at the leave hearing prepared to argue that the legal issues in this case did not deserve the attention of the Court of

Appeals. What I was not prepared for was that before I could say much, the judge told us he was going to grant leave and then spent the next half hour reminiscing with Professor Farrell about their mutual friends and acquaintances developed when the professor was a law clerk in that court.

Professor Farrell, as would be expected from an authority in the field, wrote an excellent brief to the Court of Appeals which I worked very hard to answer to the same high standard. I came to the Court of Appeals prepared for a vigorous argument but not knowing what to expect from my "old nemesis" Judge Breitel who was now the Chief Judge.

Professor Farrell, representing the side taking the appeal, was the first to argue. As is customary, he began, "May it please the Court." Unlike myself three years before, he was permitted to go on to his next sentence. But then to may utter shock and amazement, Chief Judge Breitel said, "This case involves three killings. Was your guy getting a kickback from the undertaker?" There was not much Professor Farrell could say. Everyone in the courtroom knew the case was virtually over. A few weeks later, the conviction was affirmed without opinion by the court.

A POLICE OFFICER IS MURDERED IN HIS OWN CAR

The Richard Lloyd Dennis Case

Later in 1975, I had a second case in the Court of Appeals. It was also a case I had worked on when I was in the Appeals Bureau. This case involved the murder of a police officer who was stabbed in the neck while sitting beside his partner in his parked patrol car. According to the partner, the defendant approached the car appearing to want to ask a question, but. instead, he stabbed the officer through the space created by the rolled down front passenger widow. The defendant fled as the officer's partner attended to the stabbed officer.

The defendant's fingerprints were found on the knife which was left at the scene. This led to the defendant's arrest and identification as the assailant by the partner. The main issue at the trial was whether the defendant's identity as the assailant could be established beyond a reasonable doubt.

The defendant, who was indigent, was represented by a court-appointed attorney, Albert Brackley, whose dramatic courtroom tactics and skill at poking holes in seemingly airtight testimony was well known. He also transfixed juries, because his sharp memory enabled him to conspicuously use no notes whatsoever during his trials and only twirl a paperclip between his thumb and forefinger while he cross-examined witnesses.

On appeal, in addition to the sufficiency of the identification evidence, the defendant claimed that the prosecutor's summation was overly emotional and highly inflammatory which deprived the defendant of a fair trial. The trial prosecutor was Edward Rappaport, the same person who had, four years before, been my Bureau Chief in the Investigations Bureau when I wrote a memo to him concluding that a police officer was justified in shooting a robber who had been holding a gun on the victim but neglecting to mention in the memo that the robber's gun was a toy gun. I did not forget that he had not berated me for overlooking that fact when I summarized the police reports of the case.

Thus, this case was an opportunity for me to return the favor and spare my former Bureau Chief's summation from criticism by the Court of Appeals and a finding that it required that this murder conviction being overturned.

In its decision, the Court of Appeals held that because the defendant's trial attorney did not make sufficient objections to the summation remarks, the Court of Appeals did not have the authority to review the summation comments. The court also held that the evidence of the defendant's identity as the killer was more than sufficient. This evidence included a cowboy hat found at the scene with one side folded up Australian Army style. This hat was identified by an eyewitness as the hat worn by the stabber, and an acquaintance of the defendant testified that he had seen the defendant wearing such a hat on several occasions.

This hat evidence linking the defendant to the crime would not have had much significance in Australia where these hats were far more commonly worn. But in Brooklyn, it was the 1970's equivalent of a DNA match. The odds against there being two people wearing this type of hat were intuitively significant, and, with all the other evidence in the case, the hat established the defendant's identification as the killer.

Decades later, in September 2001, when I was a judge, Mr. Brackley tried a robbery case before me. He still refrained from taking notes during the trial and still mesmerized juries by twirling a paperclip when questioning witnesses. That trial was interrupted for about a week due to the events of September 11th. Everyone re-grouped, including the jury to continue the trial. All, except the court stenographer, Chris Bini, whose firefighter husband, Carl Bini, heroically perished that day responding to the World Trade Center.

IF THE VICTIM WAS ALREADY DEAD, IT WASN'T MURDER

The Thomas Cicchetti Case

"Late in the evening of October 3, 1974, a brawl erupted into a bloodbath in the Casa Blanca Bar on Bay Ridge Avenue in Brooklyn." This was the first sentence in the Statement of Facts section of my brief and, word for word, it became the first sentence in the 1978 opinion of the Court of Appeals, my fourth homicide case in that court.

Courts have a license to repeat in their decisions without attribution the exact language used by attorneys in their legal submissions to the court. The boost to the attorney's ego when this happens, I suppose, is sufficient compensation, at least when the attorney is on the winning side.

In this case, there indeed was a brawl and a bloodbath. Four persons were either stabbed or shot and a fifth died after being both stabbed six times and shot twice, once in the head and once in the chest. The defendant was convicted of murder for being the shooter who shot the deceased in the head and thereby allegedly caused his death.

By the time I argued this case in the Court of Appeals, I was Deputy Chief of the Appeals Bureau, having completed assignments as a trial attorney in the Supreme Court Bureau, a supervisor of trial attorneys in the Narcotics Bureau, a supervisor in the Criminal Court Bureau overseeing felony cases prior to their presentation to the Grand Jury, and a supervisor of trial attorneys in the Supreme Court Bureau.

The defendant's appellate attorney in this case, Stephen Gillers, was a professor at New York University School of Law who was not much older than myself. In fact, when he was a third-year law student at N.Y.U., he was so highly regarded by the faculty that he was allowed to assist an adjunct professor to teach my freshman class in Property Law. Now, less than ten years later, I was his adversary in the Court of Appeals.

Included in the issues before the court was whether there was sufficient evidence to establish that the victim was still alive when a witness testified that the defendant approached the victim and shot him in the head. At the time, the victim was lying on the barroom floor after suffering his other injuries. If the victim was already dead, the defendant could not be convicted of killing him when he shot him in the head.

The defendant's brief argued that the evidence at trial did not sufficiently establish that the victim was alive at this time and referred the court to certain pages in the trial testimony to establish this point. However, there were other pages in the testimony that established that the deceased was alive at that time, but the defendant's brief omitted to cite those pages. I was thus in the awkward position of having to contradict my former law professor who was a noted expert in the field of legal ethics.

Recalling the embarrassing mistake I had made about the meaning of "withdrawal of a juror" in a prior appellate case, I tried to be absolutely certain that I was correct in arguing that the defendant's brief omitted to cite critical pages in the trial testimony. I stood before the Court of Appeals and made my argument with my heart in my throat.

None of the Judges took issue with me. In its decision, the court concluded that there was sufficient evidence that the deceased was alive when the defendant shot him and affirmed the conviction.

THE RISKS OF STARTING A TRIAL WITH A SICK WITNESS

The Raymond Hall Case

In 1980, Raymond Hall was charged with selling a small amount of drugs to an undercover police officer posing on the street as a drug user. Hall was arrested almost immediately after the transaction. On the day of jury selection, the undercover officer cut his finger while making an arrest in another case. There was no reason to believe he would not be available to testify at Hall's trial.

After jury selection, the trial recessed for the weekend. Because a jury had been selected, at that point "jeopardy had attached" to the defendant. This meant that the trial with this jury would have to resume to a conclusion unless there was "manifest necessity" to declare a mistrial, such as a hung jury that could not reach a verdict or a finding that the trial could not proceed in accordance with law. Otherwise, unless the defendant requested or consented to a mistrial, Fifth Amendment constitutional principles of Double Jeopardy would bar a second trial and a dismissal would result.

Over the weekend, the officer's finger became dangerously infected, and he had to be hospitalized. Although the officer was not immediately available to testify, the prosecutor assigned to the Office's Narcotics Bureau was able to call other witnesses for the first few days of the trial.

When it became clear to the trial prosecutor that he was going to run out of witnesses before the undercover officer would be released from the hospital, I received a call from the Narcotics Bureau asking for guidance. I advised the prosecutor to ask the trial judge for a continuance until the undercover officer was available and not to ask for a mistrial at the risk of a second trial being barred by the Double Jeopardy principles.

Because it was believed that the sick officer would be available within a reasonable period of time, a mistrial granted at the prosecutor's request without the consent of the defendant would enable the defendant to argue that Double Jeopardy principles would bar a second trial.

Accordingly, the prosecutor asked for a continuance of the trial and, to support his request, called the sick officer's treating physician as a witness to testify as to the undercover's condition and prospective availability. The doctor opined that "maybe" a week would be enough time, but he could not be certain.

The trial judge then ordered the prosecutor to call all the other remaining witnesses in the case. That testimony took a few more days. The prosecutor then told the trial judge that the undercover officer was the only remaining witness and that his medical condition would make him unavailable for about another week.

Defense counsel objected to a one-week adjournment, declaring that a continuance of this length would "deprive the defendant of a fair trial." Although the defendant did not specifically request a mistrial, the trial judge, nevertheless, declared a mistrial with the intention of starting a new trial with a new jury.

Where a defendant believes that a re-trial would violate the constitutional protections against Double Jeopardy, a special proceeding may be brought directly in the Appellate Division to bar the second trial. The defendant did so. Because I was familiar with the background of the case, I handled the matter for the District Attorney's Office.

The defendant argued that the trial judge was not warranted in declaring a mistrial where the defendant did not specifically ask for a mistrial. I argued that once the defendant stated that he could not receive a fair trial if the court granted the continuance requested by the prosecutor, the trial judge could not be faulted for accepting that statement to be true, and if the defendant could not get a fair trial, there was "manifest necessity" to declare a mistrial. Further, the trial judge, I argued, was entitled to accept the prosecutor's statement that the doctor believed another week was needed before the undercover officer would be available and was not required to make the doctor come back again to testify.

The defendant did not prevail in the Appellate Division and the case went to the Court of Appeals. Five appellate attorneys from the Legal Aid Society had their names on the defendant's brief that was filed with the Court of Appeals.

In the Court of Appeals, the case was the final case on that day's calendar which happened to be the last day of that particular term of the Court of Appeals. This meant that when the argument was finished, the judges were free to leave Albany for home.

My turn to argue followed the defendant's attorney, meaning I was the last lawyer to be heard that day. It was late in the afternoon and snowing. I could sense that things were going my way in the argument. I could also sense that the court was anxious for me to finish, because no judge asked me any questions as I moved from point to point in my argument. It was as if I were making a practice argument in a mirror reflecting back seven faces.

I was getting plenty of silent nods from the bench in apparent agreement with what I was saying but no questions. This was quite a contrast to my first appearance in that court where all I got was questions from Judge Breitel, who had since retired. I wrapped up my argument as quickly as I could as all seven judges seemed to smile and nod at me.

When the decision was issued, my arguments prevailed. I noticed at the end of the decision that it said the order of the Appellate Division allowing a second trial was "affirmed with costs." Because this special proceeding was civil in nature, the court had discretion to make the losing party pay certain costs incurred by prevailing party.

I had never encountered this situation and was somewhat confused, because the defendant was indigent and represented by the Legal Aid Society which obtains its funding for criminal cases from New York City. I called the Clerk of the Court of Appeals and inquired if awarding costs against the Legal Aid Society was inadvertent. I was told words to the effect that when the court awards costs to a party, it knows what it is doing.

It was decided in the District Attorney's Office not to pursue collecting these costs from the Legal Aid Society. It just would not look right and could result in harming the professionally cordial relationship between our respective offices to take their money, even if the Court of Appeals believed it would have been proper in this case.

Chapter 9. THE GRAND JURY BUREAU

Even though I enjoyed doing appellate work, I still wanted to try cases. Because I had never asked to be assigned to the Appeals Bureau, although I was fortunate to have had that experience, I felt comfortable asking for a transfer to the Grand Jury Bureau. This was where Assistants learned basic skills in questioning witnesses. Assistants who performed satisfactorily there were usually moved on to the Supreme Court Bureau to try felony cases.

The transfer came in the Spring of 1973, and I joined the group of Assistants who had been hired with me. Most of them had spent the intervening time in the Criminal Court Bureau, while I was learning how to do appellate work and handle motions in the Supreme Court.

In New York, as a general rule, a felony charge, cannot proceed to either a trial or guilty plea unless the defendant is first indicted by a grand jury. A defendant may waive the right to be indicted by a grand jury. This is ordinarily done while the felony is pending in Criminal Court early on in the case, and the defendant agrees to a plea bargain to a lesser charge.

A grand jury consists of 23 people who are called for grand jury duty in the same manner as trial jurors. A vote of only 12 of the 23 grand jurors is required to indict based on "reasonable cause to believe" the defendant committed that crime, in contrast to a trial verdict where unanimous vote of 12 is required to convict based upon a finding of "guilt beyond a reasonable doubt."

Defendants and defense attorneys are not present when a grand jury case is presented. Neither is a judge present. The prosecutor serves as the legal advisor to the grand jury. Witnesses are called one at a time and testify under oath in answer to questions asked by the prosecutor. The proceeding is essentially a presentation of the prosecution's case with no cross-examination of the witnesses by the defendant's attorney. Defendants have a right to testify if they request to do so, in which case they are asked questions by the prosecutor after making their statement to the grand jury.

Defendant's rarely elect to testify, because the standard needed to indict is much lower than the standard needed to convict at a trial. Further, because a defendant is not present during grand jury proceedings, a defendant would have to testify without knowing the details of the prosecution's case. It is, therefore, the general belief that defendants should reserve the opportunity to give their side of the story until the trial which would be after they have heard the prosecution's witnesses testify and where the burden of proof needed to convict is much higher than the burden of proof needed to just indict. Also, if a defendant testifies in the grand jury and is indicted, the prosecution will know in advance what the defendant's testimony will be at the trial and have months to prepare to refute it.

When I was assigned to the grand jury, there were approximately 12,000 indictments a year voted in Brooklyn. Broken down, this meant there were over 200 new indictments voted each week. Cases were presented to five separate grand juries which sat five days a week for four weeks at a time, after which they were replaced by a new set of grand jurors.

There were about 20 Assistants assigned to the Grand Jury Bureau to present over 90 percent of these cases which were eventually handled by either the Supreme Court or Narcotics Bureaus following the filing of an indictment. The remaining cases were presented by Assistants in the Homicide Bureau or the

Rackets Bureau, which handled major frauds and the few organized crime cases that were not otherwise prosecuted in federal court.

Under the law at that time, a defendant arrested for a felony who was incarcerated in lieu of posting bail had to be, within 144 hours of being arrested, either indicted and have the completed indictment filed, or held for grand jury action after a preliminary hearing in Criminal Court, or be released. Preliminary hearings, as a matter of Office policy, were not held, because these hearings required witnesses to testify and be cross-examined by the defense and then, if the judge at the preliminary hearing determined that the defendant's commission of a felony was sufficiently established, the witnesses would have to testify again in the grand jury. Thus, if the witnesses were available, felony cases would be presented directly to the grand jury without a preliminary hearing.

Therefore, not only was the volume of grand jury cases per Assistant high, there was also time pressure on the Assistants in cases where the defendants were incarcerated, which usually were the more serious cases involving violent crimes, to finish presenting the case and file a completed indictment before the law required that the defendant be released. Several years later, this law was slightly modified to require the voting of only a single count of the indictment, rather than a complete grand jury presentation and the filing of an actual indictment in order to meet the 144-hour release deadline.

The volume of cases and the need to expeditiously process them provided an opportunity for Assistants to either learn how to do it under pressure or realize that they were not cut out for this type of work.

Witnesses in grand jury cases were notified by District Attorney office staff to appear on the day the case was scheduled for presentation. The witnesses reported to a large room with rows of bench seats. There was a counter at the front of the room where the witnesses reported to a clerk who kept attendance as witnesses reported on each case. When all the witnesses on a case had appeared, the papers on the case were placed at section of the counter called "the deck." Assistants who were ready to start a new case were supposed to go to the deck and pick up the next case in line without looking through the papers to see what the case was about. Ducking a case with a problem was frowned upon.

The Assistant would then look at the papers which usually had nothing more than a copy of the complaint filed in Criminal Court and the defendant's criminal record, if any. Next, the Assistant would escort the witnesses into a small office, ask them some questions about the case, briefly explain that the grand jury process was not a trial, that the defendant would not be there, and that the Assistant would be asking them as few questions as possible with the purpose of establishing the basic facts about what happened.

Usually not all the potential witnesses in the case were notified to appear, because their names were not noted in the file if they had not given statements to the police. It was up the Assistant in the grand jury to determine the identities of not only the essential witnesses, but also the identities of the potential witnesses, who could support, or possibly contradict, the witnesses named in the file. These additional witnesses might be interviewed by the assigned Assistant in the Supreme Court Bureau after the indictment was filed if their existence was discovered, and if they were willing to cooperate.

Not speaking with all possible witnesses and having complete information about the facts of the case is, perhaps, the leading cause of both failed prosecutions as well as unjust prosecutions of the innocent. As we all know, witnesses to crimes, especially if they are not personally involved, do not always come forward and volunteer to tell the police or the attorneys what they know. Further, while the prosecution is duty-bound to disclose favorable information to the defense, the defense is ethically prohibited from disclosing to the prosecution information unfavorable to the defense.

If both sides had equal access to all of the relevant information in a case, the truth would be more readily ascertainable. Instead, each side has to work to discover who knows what about the case, and that search is not always successful.

The mission of the Assistants in the grand jury was to present the case and obtain an indictment for a felony if the facts as known could establish that a felony was committed. If the felony charge was not "serious," such as where the injuries were minor or the amount stolen barely exceeded the felony threshold of $250 (it has since been legislatively raised to $1,000), the Assistant could seek permission from the Grand Jury Bureau Chief or Deputy Bureau Chief to have the case prosecuted as a misdemeanor in Criminal Court.

One of the five sitting grand juries was known as "the quick deck." It was reserved for the presentation of narcotics cases where the only witnesses were police officers. Felony narcotics cases consisted mostly of street sales to undercover police officers posing as narcotics buyers. A sale of any amount of a narcotic drug, such as heroin or cocaine, is a felony, and the majority of these cases involved sales in amounts of $20 worth or less.

The only memorable case I handled during my five months in the grand jury was a case involving an alleged rape of a young woman by her boyfriend. I don't remember if the case was based on the boyfriend's use of force or on the girlfriend's being below the age of consent. Although an arrest had been made, the evidence consisted solely of the girlfriend's testimony about what happened. There were no other witnesses to what allegedly happened or any medical or scientific evidence. The law at the time was that this evidence was insufficient, because there was no corroboration of the girlfriend's testimony.

After looking at the file and speaking with the girlfriend, I then spoke with her father to explain why the case could not be prosecuted. I carefully explained the law to him and gave him examples of what types of evidence would be needed in addition to his daughter's testimony. After going through this explanation, including mentioning that the boyfriend did not make any admissions to the police or to any other person as far as was known, the father said something like, "Well, what if he admitted to me that he raped her?" I asked him to tell me the details of this purported admission and how he came to talk with the boyfriend about this after the boyfriend was arrested. His explanation made no sense and seemed tailored to meet my explanation of the evidence that was needed in the case.

I reported this to my Bureau Chief, and he asked that I bring the father in to speak with him. The Bureau Chief, Al Koch, a seasoned prosecutor who was adept at teaching young Assistants how to analyze the legal aspects of a case, then showed me how to handle the human aspects of this case. He expressed to the father his sympathy for what happened to his daughter and his disagreement with the state of the law in New York that required her testimony to be corroborated.

63

He then also said that if the father testified falsely about the defendant making an admission, the District Attorney's Office would prosecute the father for perjury which would only make the bad situation for his daughter worse. The father understood and retracted his statement about what he claimed the boyfriend said to him.

Through presentation of hundreds of cases, I learned how to ask witnesses legally proper questions and listen to the answers in order to frame appropriate follow-up questions. All too often lawyers just ask their witness a prepared list of questions knowing how the witness has previously answered the question and do not perceive that the actual testimony differs and needs amplification or clarification.

Although from my prior experience in the Appeals Bureau I had read dozens of trial and grand jury transcripts so as to become familiar with the rules for asking a legally proper question, there is nothing like the practical experience of doing it with live witnesses before a live "audience" to sharpen the skill of doing it on your own.

Chapter 10. *TRYING CASES IN THE SUPREME COURT*

"Ladies and Gentlemen of the jury." When I said those words for the first time before a real jury in my first trial, I knew it was a thrill I would not forget. Joining a prosecutor's office directly out of law school provides an excellent opportunity to acquire "trial experience," and that was one of my hopes when I joined the Office. This proved to be true, when after about two years in the District Attorney's Office, I, along with several other Assistant District Attorneys who had started when I did, had progressed to the point where we were transferred out of the Grand Jury Bureau and assigned to the Supreme Court Bureau to try felony cases.

At the time, the Supreme Court Bureau handled the felonies that were not assigned to the Homicide, Narcotics, or Rackets Bureaus. The proliferation of specialized trial bureaus, such as Sex Crimes, Economic Crimes, Domestic Violence, Law Enforcement Investigations, and others that exist today did not occur until the next decade in the 1980's. For the most part, these categories of cases fell into the general mix of assault, robbery, auto larceny, and gun possession cases that were the grist of the Supreme Court Bureau's workload.

At the time, judges in the Supreme Court had their own calendars of over a hundred cases each, and there were two Assistant District Attorneys assigned to each judge's court part. Usually, the two Assistants alternated trying cases. The Assistant who was not on trial handled the calendar calls of the other cases and prepared the next case scheduled for trial. Each court part had a District Attorney's Office Detective Investigator, known as "DI's," assigned to help the two Assistants contact witnesses, serve subpoenas, obtain documents, and keep track of the case files. DI's were not members of the City's police department but had some law enforcement training and were authorized to carry a gun and make arrests.

There was no such thing as computer record keeping. Each file had a "trial sheet" - an approximately 20 x 15 inch heavy duty paper sheet - with the name of the case, the indictment number and the charges. The result of each court appearance was supposed to be recorded on the trial sheet which was how the Office kept track of the next court date for each case. When the case was completed, the trial sheet was filed in a central office and a handwritten entry reflecting the disposition was made in an oversized log book on a page designated for that case when the indictment was filed. The District Attorney's Office had scores of these books going back over a hundred years.

The Court system also kept its records by hand in similar log books. Because all of these records were kept by hand and entries in the books were not made contemporaneously with the event to be recorded, no one ever knew exactly how many cases were pending at a given time.

In the Supreme Court Bureau, there was no intermediate level of supervision between the "line Assistants" and the Bureau and Deputy Bureau Chief. Assistants would go directly to them, depending on which one of them was available, with any questions they had concerning their cases. After answering the questions, the bosses would occasionally write a note on the file flap reflecting their instructions if it concerned whether a particular plea offer had been authorized. Woe be it to the Assistant who missed or intentionally disregarded that note on the file flap that may have been put there when the case was assigned to another Assistant.

Soon after my start in the Supreme Court Bureau, the Office decided to create the position of "Trial Supervisor" to serve as a direct supervisor of Assistants in the Supreme Court and Narcotics Bureaus. This supervisor would be more readily available to answer questions as they came up during the day and have the time to observe Assistants in the court to provide on-going advice and first-hand evaluation. My Trial Supervisor was a few years older than myself and an experienced trial lawyer. His advice was always helpful, but sometimes he was notoriously unavailable when his office door was locked. It was rumored it had something to do with the couch in his office - and it was not because he was napping.

There was no formal training program on either the law or trial techniques. Unbelievable as it may seem, knowledge was passed informally by word of mouth, including fundamental legal concepts, such as which side goes first at a pre-trial hearing to suppress evidence, or what questions should a prosecutor ask potential jurors during the jury selection process. This is where my one year in the Appeals Bureau reading trial transcripts and actually looking at a law book to find an answer to a question made me a valuable resource to my colleagues. As they say, "In the land of the blind, the one-eyed man in king."

I had about 15 trials in the Supreme Court Bureau before being promoted to the Narcotics Bureau to be the Trial Supervisor for that bureau. This move came as a surprise, because I had never tried a narcotics case which had its own unique scenarios, such as "buy and busts" (involving undercover officers making drug buys on the street followed by immediate arrests of the sellers) and "observation sales" (street drug sales observed through binoculars by officers hiding on rooftops where both the drug buyer and seller are arrested).

None of my Supreme Court Bureau trials were particularly unique, but some of them were memorable for their own reasons, although I do not recall the names of the defendants.

A SHOOTING IN A QUIET NEIGHBORHOOD

My first trial involved a shooting by a man who was in his home in Bay Ridge one afternoon when he heard his daughter screaming outside in front of his house. His daughter had been driving with her boyfriend when the boyfriend and the eventual shooting victim became involved in some kind of road rage incident. Apparently, the boyfriend then deliberately damaged the victim's car and tried to drive away. The victim pursued in his own car. The boyfriend drove to his girlfriend's home and parked about half a block away.

The girlfriend and boyfriend got out of their car and ran towards her home with the girlfriend screaming for help. The victim parked his car and ran down the block after them. The girl's father heard the screams, grabbed his licensed pistol, and went outside to see his daughter standing outside and the victim pursuing the boyfriend, both running towards the father.

The father, not having a chance to learn what was going on, shot the victim as he was fighting with the boyfriend in the street. The victim survived and recovered from his wound, but a bullet remained lodged near his spinal cord where it was too risky for the surgeons to try to remove it.

It was really the boyfriend who was the instigator in this case for provoking the incident. But he was not on trial, and the jury needed someone to blame for the victim's injuries. The father's defense was that, based on the rapidly occurring events as they appeared to him, he believed his use of a gun was reasonably necessary to defend his daughter or her boyfriend, and, therefore the shooting was justified. The jury, nevertheless, found the defendant guilty.

It is not commonly known that when a defense of "justification" - meaning self-defense or defense of another person - is raised at a trial by a defendant, the defendant does not have the burden to prove he acted in self-defense. Rather, the prosecution must prove beyond a reasonable doubt that the defendant's actions were not justified, which, in a close case, means the defendant gets "the benefit of the doubt." However, in this case, there was no evidence that the victim had a weapon or was about to cause serious physical injury to anyone when the defendant shot him. Thus, the defendant was convicted even though this was all brought about by his daughter and her boyfriend who were not charged with anything.

The memorable part for me is what happened before the trial. I had never previously tried a case before a jury. The few trials I had in Criminal Court were non-jury trials before a single judge sitting as the trier of fact. I also had never seen a jury selected. I was flying blind here.

I had read about a dozen full trial records while in the Appeals Bureau, so I had some idea of the procedures to be followed during the trial. But I had absolutely no experience in the procedures involved in selecting a jury.

This part of the trial was usually not transcribed and not part of the appellate record, because it was not until the 1980's that appellate court decisions bared attorneys from selecting jurors based on their race, gender, or ethnicity. Thereafter, this part of the trial was also routinely transcribed so it could be reviewed on appeal.

The more experienced Assistant assigned to the Part with me was supposed to sit next to me at counsel table during the trial and serve as an advisor. The Trial Supervisor position had not yet been created, so I had no other resource. Sadly, this Assistant had a serious drinking problem and usually spent his lunch hours in a bar. On one occasion I had to join him there in order to get some questions answered.

Prior to jury selection, I obtained from a book of "scripts" kept by the Supreme Court Bureau a "cheat sheet" of sample questions to ask jurors during the jury selection process. I was planning on using this script and whatever help my colleague would provide. However, on the afternoon jury selection was to begin, my colleague did not return to court from the bar.

This case had some difficult issues from a prosecutor's point of view, such as a sympathetic defendant with no criminal record who had charming daughter and a victim who appeared to have fully recovered from being shot.

As a result of a change in the Criminal Procedure Law controlling the jury selection process, the trial judge now initiates the questioning of potential jurors by introducing the parties, instructing the jurors on their basic functions and responsibilities, and obtaining basic biographical information from them. But at the time of this trial, it was the prosecutor who initiated the questioning and performed these functions. Using the script, I somehow got through the process and a jury was selected, although I believe I was so obviously nervous and unsure of myself that virtually everyone in the courtroom not only knew it, but also felt sorry for me.

After the verdict convicting the defendant, I had an opportunity to speak with some of the jurors in the hallway outside their jury room to thank them for their service. I proudly told them this was my first trial. As a group, they answered with smiles, "We could tell."

A SURPRISE WITNESS FOR THE PROSECUTION

Although a defendant charged with a felony has a right to a jury trial, the law allows the defendant the choice to waive a jury and, instead, have the case tried by a judge. There can be many tactical reasons for this choice, including a decision that the case will be decided on "technical" legal issues rather than on the usual factual questions concerning "what happened" or "who done it."

For example, in some assault cases, the facts concerning what happened and who did it may not be in dispute, but there may be uncertainty whether the defendant, despite the severity of the injury, actually intended to cause serious physical injury to the victim, which may be the basis for the most serious charge. Sometimes the defense would prefer that a judge rather than a jury make that decision, particularly when the defense believes the jury's sympathy with the victim would affect their decision.

I prosecuted such an assault case where the defendant had waived a jury. The trial judge, the Hon. John Ryan, was known for his patience, courtesy, and excellent judicial temperament. It was one of my first trials and my wife, who was in the neighborhood of the courthouse that day, dropped in and was sitting in the audience.

The victim testified that he had sustained an injury to his left arm during an altercation with the defendant. I had obtained a certified copy of his hospital records reflecting the treatment for his injuries, and the records were accepted in evidence without the need for anyone from the hospital to explain what they were. Once the records were accepted into evidence, I was entitled to read from them, and I read a portion to the court.

When I came to the part describing the injuries, I read "left arm." The defendant's attorney objected to my reading the word "left" because instead of stating "left," the record actually contained the letter "L" with a circle around it. No one took this as a legally crucial objection, because there was no dispute that the victim's left arm had been injured. Judge Ryan, obviously knowing that the circled "L" meant "left," nevertheless, sustained the objection and ruled I was not qualified to interpret the meaning of the circled "L."

It was apparent that the defense attorney and the judge were having a little fun at my expense and that this by-play was not going to affect the outcome of the case. However, I saw an opportunity, since there was no jury to be distracted by the informality of what was taking place, to continue this brief departure from what was, of course, a serious proceeding.

I asked for permission to call an "expert witness" on the meaning of a circled "L" in the medical records. I said there was a registered nurse in the audience with many years of experience in reading medical records in numerous hospitals and that if defense counsel would not agree that the circled "L" in this case meant "left," I should be allowed to call this witness to give an opinion on the question. I also stated that this "expert" happened to be my wife.

As much as my request surprised the judge and defense counsel, my wife was the most surprised person in the courtroom when she heard that I was going to call her as a witness. The judge and defense counsel both agreed that she could be called as a witness. After all, they were both responsible for making an issue out of this virtually indisputable notation.

My wife, grasping that this was not really a meaningful part of the trial and, I guess, not wanting to embarrass me by refusing, took the witness stand and was sworn in by the court clerk. I asked her some brief questions about her experience with medical records and then asked the judge, based on that experience, to permit her to give her "expert" opinion on the meaning of the circled "L" in these records. Without objection by the defense, the judge ruled she was sufficiently qualified as an expert to give her opinion. She answered that it meant "left." There was no cross-examination.

The defendant was convicted, but I do not recall whether it was for the most serious crimes he was charged with. I do know that this was the last time my wife came to a courtroom to watch me prosecute a case.

RAPES IN THE PARK

Victims and their families suffer when the crime is committed, and if there is a trial and an acquittal reflecting that the jury did not believe the victim, that is the very definition of adding insult to injury - even if the acquittal is warranted by the evidence in the case. Further, the prosecutor who unsuccessfully tried the case cannot but also feel the additional pain caused to the victim by the acquittal. This trial was over 40 years ago, but the verdict still haunts me.

The teenage boyfriend and girlfriend were in Prospect Park late one evening engaged in a romantic interlude. The 16-year-old girl was slightly below 17, the age where she could legally consent, making what the slightly older boyfriend was doing a misdemeanor.

At trial, she testified she was a virgin before that night. The macho boyfriend, when he later testified, recalled that they, in fact, had intercourse several times prior to that night. This is not what the trial was about, but, no doubt, this testimony did not win the boyfriend any points with the jury.

Both teenagers testified that they were accosted in the park by two young men with knives who tied up the boyfriend and each then had intercourse with the girlfriend while the boyfriend watched. When the two men left, the girlfriend untied her boyfriend and they both reported what happened to the police. The police had them separately look through mug shot photo books containing the photographs of people who had been arrested in other cases. They each separately picked out the same two photographs out of the hundreds of photographs they viewed.

Both men were arrested and placed in separate lineups containing themselves and five other men who were of the same general height, weight, age, and facial appearance. The boyfriend and girlfriend each separately viewed the two lineups and each separately identified the two men whose photographs they had separately selected.

Because the boyfriend was a witness to the entire event and identified each defendant as a participant, the case had the full corroboration of the victim's testimony that the then-existing law required. There was no scientific evidence connecting either defendant to the crime. The police did not go to the crime scene to try to find fingerprints of the perpetrators. The victim was not given a sexual assault examination at the hospital to attempt to find forensic evidence such as DNA or hair of the perpetrators. These hospital procedures were not in place as a matter of routine as they are today, and DNA evidence was unheard of at that time.

The defendants through their attorneys argued at trial that both witnesses were mistaken in their identifications of them.

As the prosecutor, I had three problems to overcome. First, I could not show that the two defendants even knew each other, no less committed the crime together. They did not live in the same neighborhood. School records were checked, and they never went to the same school.

Second, the law in New York, which differs from most other states, does not allow a jury to hear testimony about a witness's prior photographic identification of a defendant. The essential reason is a judicially expressed belief that if a jury learns the police have a prior photograph of the defendant, the jury will infer that the photograph was taken when the defendant was arrested in a prior case thereby causing undue prejudice to the defendant in the case on trial. Therefore, the jury at this trial did not know that the two witnesses separately picked the same two photographs out of hundreds of photographs, greatly reducing the odds of a mistake as compared to the two witnesses picking the same two people out of a lineup of six people.

The third problem was that while the girlfriend testified in a straightforward manner and held up under cross-examination regarding her ability to make an accurate identification, the boyfriend came across as somewhat of a wise guy, probably due, in part, to his being embarrassed about not being able to have prevented what happened and, in part, due to his having to admit to having sex with a minor. The problems with the boyfriend as a witness logically should not have mattered, because the girlfriend testified to the same things, including her separate identifications of both defendants.

After the jury heard the summations from the two defense attorneys and me, the trial judge instructed the jury on the legal principles involved in the case, including the legal requirement, which does not exist today, that the victim's testimony about being raped be fully corroborated by other evidence. The jury then retired to deliberate on its verdict. The jury returned a verdict of not guilty as to both defendants.

I took the opportunity to speak with some of the jurors in the hallway after the verdict to ask them what they thought about the case. Debating with jurors at this point is improper and could be viewed as a violation of ethical rules. I just wanted to hear what they had to say about the case.

What I was told was, in substance, that, the jury believed the victim and that her identification was correct but that they had doubts about the boyfriend's testimony and, therefore, the victim's testimony was not sufficiently corroborated. As I was trying to absorb how the jury could find that two people can say the same thing but only one of them be correct, one of the jurors added that during deliberations another juror had said that the boyfriend was probably a gang member, because that juror had grown up in the same neighborhood and, at that time, "everyone" was a gang member.

Some lawyers have said that speaking to jurors after the case to learn the reasons for their verdict is a waste of time, because jurors really never disclose the true reasons for their verdict. Sometimes, if the verdict is based on an unconscious bias, they may not even know why they were persuaded. You only hear what jurors feel comfortable telling other people after the fact. In this case, I wish I had never asked.

"A 68 YEAR-OLD WOMAN AND A 14 YEAR-OLD GIRL"

The defendant in this case was a large man in his late 20's. He had been confined in lieu of posting bail for about two years since his arrest, about a year of which consisted of confinement in a psychiatric prison facility, because he was mentally "not fit to proceed." This meant that due a mental problem he was either unable to understand the charges or cooperate with his attorney in assisting in his defense.

After being given massive doses Thorazine, an anti-psychotic drug, in addition to whatever else was done for him by the doctors at the facility, he was deemed fit to proceed in their opinion and his attorney did not contest that finding. Still, to me as he appeared in court he seemed very heavily medicated.

The defendant was charged with breaking into an apartment where a 68 year-old grandmother was babysitting for her 10 year-old grandson and her 14 year-old granddaughter. At knifepoint the defendant ordered the two women into the bedroom. The defendant apparently did not notice the boy who was hiding behind a curtain throughout the incident.

According to the testimony of both women, the defendant ordered them to take off their clothes and get into the double bed. The defendant then pulled down his pants and, while holding the knife to one woman, had intercourse with the other. He then got off the first woman and had intercourse with the second woman while holding the knife to the neck of the first woman. As this was happening, the children's mother returned home from work and walked in on this scene. The defendant jumped out of the bed, pulled up his pants, grabbed a small television set that was on the dresser, and ran out of the apartment.

The police were called. A report was taken. The grandmother and granddaughter were brought to a hospital for an examination. The witnesses all gave a description of the person they saw, but no identifications were made.

About a week later while playing in the street, the boy who had been hiding behind the curtain saw the defendant on the street and recognized him as the person who had been in his apartment. He ran home and told his mother. The mother then went outside and recognized him too. She called the police and the defendant was arrested. The grandmother and granddaughter were also present at the scene of the arrest and identified the defendant as well.

Even though four witnesses identified the defendant, whose large size was a most distinguishing feature, the defense at trial was that all of the witnesses were mistaken. The defense argued that once the boy mistakenly identified the defendant and this became known to the other witnesses, their identifications were not based on their independent recollections of the perpetrator, but, rather, were influenced by their knowledge that someone else had identified the defendant. The defense argued that it was the defendant's large size that was identified and not his face, because each of the witnesses never really got a good look at the face of the perpetrator.

Shortly before the trial began, I put in a rush order to obtain the victims' hospital records which had not been ordered by the prior Assistants assigned to the case. The records were delivered to the courtroom on the last day of the trial which only lasted about three days including one day for jury selection. On looking at the records, I was shocked to see that, as to each victim, the records stated that a vaginal examination showed no evidence of their having had intercourse. I had no other witnesses and rested my case.

I turned the records over to defense counsel as was my obligation, because the records contained information helpful to the defense. The defense attorney never expected this result and had been content to have the case tried without the medical records, because he believed the records would support prosecution's case rather than contradict it. The defense offered the medical records in evidence and rested the defense case.

The defense summation argued that the witnesses were mistaken in their identifications and, further, not only did the medical records show there had been no rapes of the two women, but also their other testimony, as well as the testimony of the boy and his mother, should not be credited.

My summation essentially said that the evidence showed that the identifications were accurate and that the identifications of the adults would not have been influenced by the knowing that a 10-year-old had first made an identification. Further, when the mother walked into the bedroom she had an excellent opportunity to observe the defendant as he was putting on his pants, grabbing the television set, and passing right in front of her as he left the bedroom

But to save the case, I knew I had to explain why the medical records showed no evidence of intercourse even though the two women said the defendant had been on top of them with his pants down and moving his hips. I came up with an explanation, but I knew it was a borderline legal question whether I could give that explanation in the absence of specific evidence at the trial to support my argument.

I decided not to ask the trial judge for an advance ruling and take my chances. Referring to the absence of medical evidence of rape, I said to the jury, "Any man who would want to have simultaneous sexual relations with a 68 year-old woman and a 14 year-old girl has a sexual problem, and isn't it a symptom of that problem that he could not get an erection?"

As soon as I said those words while standing facing the jury box, I heard the judge sitting at the bench behind me raise his voice and say, "There was no evidence about that at this trial. The jury is to disregard that remark." I quickly concluded my summation.

After deliberating, the jury found the defendant not guilty of the rapes but convicted him of Robbery in the First Degree for taking the television while threatening the use of a knife. A conviction on that charge carried the same 25 year sentence as the rape charges, which, based on the medical records, the jury found the defendant did not commit.

Once again, I spoke to some of the jurors after the verdict. They were all totally convinced the defendant was correctly identified and expressed their sympathies to all of the witnesses for what they went through in this case. For whatever it may be worth, one of the jurors said, "You know that thing you said that the judge told us to disregard. You had a good point."

"CROSS-EXAMINING" THE TRIAL JUDGE

In the Summer of 1974, I had been in the Supreme Court Bureau for less than a year when, due to an extensive trial backlog in the Homicide Bureau, I was assigned a murder case to try. Naturally, a relatively inexperienced Assistant such as myself was not going to be given a murder case that the Homicide Bureau would want to keep for its own Assistants.

I soon saw why this case was "dumped" on me, but I really didn't mind, because I was going to have an opportunity to try a murder case in less than three years in the Office. Having already briefed and argued a homicide case in the Court of Appeals, I was going to achieve a rare, if not singularly unique, accomplishment of also trying a murder case in less than three years in the Office.

The case involved a shotgun shooting on a staircase in a brownstone building. The deceased was a large young man with a reputation as the neighborhood tough guy. The defendant lived in the building and was a slightly built young man. According to the eyewitness testimony, the defendant and the deceased were on the street in front of the brownstone where the deceased was verbally abusing the defendant and threatening him with physical harm. They were known to each other from the neighborhood, and the deceased had previously been abusive towards the defendant, which I contended gave the defendant a motive to kill him.

After this episode of abuse, the defendant went into his apartment and obtained a shotgun. He left the apartment and was walking down the stairs heading towards the street when he confronted the deceased on the staircase and shot him with both barrels causing his death.

The defendant contended he obtained the shotgun only to scare the deceased and did not expect to confront the deceased inside the building. When he saw the deceased, the defendant testified he believed the defendant was following him into the building in order to carry out a verbal threat he had just made on the street. Having nowhere to flee on the staircase, the defendant fired at the deceased believing this was necessary to save his own life from an attack by a much larger man.

Certainly, the defendant's version had several weak points that were ripe for cross-examination, such as why was he going back out on the street with a shotgun and whether he really believed he had to shoot the deceased in order to save his own life. The problem with cross-examining the defendant, however, was not only did he have a very heavy southern drawl, he also had a speech impediment that made it very difficult for him to be understood while he testified.

To address this problem, particularly so the court reporter could understand the defendant and prepare an accurate transcript of his testimony, the trial judge repeated every word of the defendant's testimony. Thus, the jury heard the defendant's self-serving answers in the defendant's own voice and then again in the voice of the trial judge, complete with the judge's own dramatic shifts in tone of voice depending on the context of what the defendant was saying. Perhaps if I had more experience, although I am sure no one had ever had experience in this situation, I would have asked the trial judge not to try to imitate the defendant's voice inflections when repeating his testimony. Where a witness does not speak English, an official court interpreter is used to translate the questions, which the witness answers in his own language, and then the interpreter translates the answer. There really is no other way to do it. However, the jury gets to hear the English translation only once, and it is in the voice of the interpreter. In this case, the jury heard the witnesses answers twice: once from the witness and again from the authoritative voice of the trial judge who assumed the persona of the defendant. I believe this made it more difficult for the jury to doubt the defendant's believability and may have influenced the jury to find the shooting was justified in self-defense.

This is not to say that the acquittal was not based on the evidence in the case. One of the important facts in the case was how far apart the defendant and the deceased were when the defendant fired the shotgun. The closer they were, the more the deceased represented an actual and immediate physical threat to the defendant. The further apart, the more the defendant would have had an opportunity to flee rather than fire the shotgun in self-defense. The autopsy of the deceased showed that in addition to the shotgun wounds, the body of the deceased contained shotgun wadding, which is a sort of packing material for the pellets in a shotgun shell. The presence of wadding in the body of the deceased indicated the two were close when the shotgun was fired.

"How close?" was the question I asked the Medical Examiner who performed the autopsy. This conversation took place in the hallway outside the courtroom just before he testified. The Medical Examiner was the Chief Medical Examiner in Kings County and later served as the Chief Medical Examiner of the City of New York. His credentials were impeccable. His answer was, "How close do you want them?" I was stunned to think that he would tailor his testimony to help my case. But maybe he was not serious and just wanted to test my integrity to see if I would feed him an answer that would help me. While in the Appeals Bureau, I had read several trial records in homicide cases where he testified about autopsies he had performed. I knew he was very smart and very experienced. I hoped he not was serious when he asked me that question, but I never really learned. I told him that I just wanted his opinion and that I would work with whatever his answer would be. He gave me a range of distances from the tip of the barrel of the shotgun to the body of the deceased that indicated that the two men were likely less than 10 feet apart and later testified to that. I am sure the jury took this distance into account in deciding the defendant was not guilty.

PART II. PRESIDING OVER FELONY TRIALS

As noted in the Introduction, after being appointed a Criminal Court Judge in 1987 and subsequently being designated an Acting Supreme Court Justice in 1992, I was privileged to preside over almost 500 felony trials until I retired at the end of 2015. The following, separated by category, are summaries of some of the trials I presided over between 2008 and 2015. These trials are not unlike many of the cases tried every day in our City's courts and their stories, though largely unpublicized, provide some insight into how these real cases are resolved in our court system.

Chapter 11. *SEX CRIMES TRIALS*

A NAKED MAN RUNNING THROUGH THE STREETS

People v. Chance McCurdy (5964/11)

This defendant had pled guilty to a sex crimes charge before me several years before, and it was just a coincidence that his new case was sent to me for trial. At the time of this incident, the defendant was a registered sex offender. The jury did know any of this, because, generally, a defendant's prior criminal record is not admissible in evidence to establish that the defendant has a propensity to commit similar crimes.

In this unusual case, the victim, a male in his early 20's, was approached on the street by the defendant at 4:00 am, and at knifepoint, the victim was ordered into the courtyard of a brownstone. With his back to the ground floor door, the victim was ordered to take off all his clothes. The defendant then pulled down his own pants and told the victim to "suck his dick." With the

84

defendant's pants now at his ankles, the victim, although completely naked, was able to push past the defendant and run home, a distance of several blocks.

Video surveillance obtained by the police showed the victim running naked through the empty streets. If you ever wondered if you were in this situation whether you would run with your hands covering your genitals or choose to run faster with your hands at your sides, you may be interested in knowing that the victim in this case chose the more modest, but slower, running style.

When he arrived home, the victim told his mother and sister what had happened. They all went back to the scene to recover the victim's clothing and cell phone.

The clothing was there, but instead of the victim's cell phone, another cell phone was found on the ground. The defendant had apparently taken the victim's cell phone, because several days later, the defendant was shown on video surveillance in a T-Mobile store switching the victim's cell phone to his mother's cell phone account.

The jury acquitted the defendant of forcibly stealing the cell phone, which was the robbery charge, but found the defendant guilty of the lesser charge of petit larceny for taking the cell phone without using force. On the charge of attempting to engage in a criminal sexual act with the victim, which carried a maximum 15-year sentence, the jury was deadlocked and could not reach a verdict. The jury may have suspected there was more to the story than what the victim was willing to reveal, particularly in view of the victim's somewhat confused account of where he had been earlier that night before this happened.

Rather than try this case again to resolve the attempted sexual act charge on which the jury could not agree, the District Attorney's Office reached a plea arrangement with the defense. The defendant pleaded guilty to that charge in return for the prosecution recommending sentence of probation, which is what I imposed, in addition to a year in jail for taking the cell phone which the defendant had already served while awaiting trial.

HE CALLED HIMSELF "THE DEVIL"

People v. Carlos Hairston (2555/11)

The defendant was charged with the forcible sexual assault of two different women under a relatively new statute that carried a potential life sentence for committing a sexual assault after previously committing another sexual assault. As worded, the statute did not require a previous "conviction" for sexual assault, but, rather, only previously "committing" a sexual assault. Thus, the two pending sexual assault cases involving different victims could be be tried together. Guilty verdicts for both sexual assaults would be required for a conviction for this single charge.

Prior to the enactment of that statute, a defendant would be entitled to attempt to persuade the trial judge to order that the two cases be tried separately on the ground that hearing evidence of one case would interfere with the jury's ability to separately consider the evidence of guilt on the other case. But this new statute made evidence of one crime an element of the other crime, so it would, therefore, be necessary for the jury to hear proof of both crimes.

The defendant had moved to New York from Ohio. He was a black Orthodox Jew who dressed in Hasidic garb: black suit, long black coat, and a large black fedora-style hat. In the first case, he met the victim at 2:00 am in a Harlem subway station. Video surveillance showed most of their encounter.

The victim testified that at the time she was 9-months pregnant and had been thrown out of her apartment by her mother after an argument. The victim asked to borrow the defendant's telephone to try to call her mother. She called but could not reach her. The defendant and the victim eventually travelled on a subway to Brooklyn where the defendant told her he lived and would allow her to stay with him. The victim testified she trusted the defendant because of his Hasidic clothing.

The defense argued to the jury that the victim, in fact, was a prostitute. The defense argued that a man seen in the background of the subway surveillance video was her pimp based on the way he was lingering at the station and pacing back and forth while looking at the victim and the defendant who were in conversation. The victim in her testimony denied she was a prostitute and denied having any relationship with the man shown in the video.

On reaching Brooklyn, the two exited the subway and walked into an alley where the defendant said his apartment door was located. He then came at her from behind and started choking her while telling her he would kill her if she screamed. He ordered her to undress, placed his penis in her mouth, and then he placed his penis in her anus. When he was finished, she cleaned herself with wipes she had in her pocketbook. The defendant took the wipes from her and put them in his pocket. He left and told her not to scream, because he would be watching her and kill her if she did. She put her clothes back on and walked to a nearby corner. She told a security guard there at a construction site to call the police.

Twelve days later, in a different part of Brooklyn where the defendant actually lived, the second victim was accosted by the defendant as she was walking home from the subway. Unlike the first victim who came from a troubled personal situation, the second victim was educated and employed in an office job in Manhattan. She had recently arrived in New York from her family's home in the mid-west.

After meeting some friends after work for drinks, she took the subway home to Brooklyn and was walking there from the station. On the sidewalk, she passed a black man dressed as an Orthodox Jew, which she noted because she had never seen this before.

As she entered her building, she was grabbed from behind by the man she had just passed on the sidewalk. He covered her mouth and told her that if she screamed, he would kill her. He forced her down the stairs to a basement laundry room. He ordered her to undress and told her "he was the devil and this is what he does." He touched her breasts with his hand and mouth. She said he did not have to do this and that they could pray together. This seemed to anger him. He forced her to her knees and put his penis in her mouth. He then told her to turn around and put her hands on the floor. When she did this, he vaginally penetrated her from behind with his penis.

DNA was recovered from both crime scenes and found to match the defendant's DNA. To further identify the defendant as the perpetrator of the first crime, the jury was shown still photographs taken from the subway surveillance video of the man talking to the first victim to compare to the defendant's appearance in the courtroom.

The defendant testified and did not dispute his identification as the person in the subway station who had sex with the first victim. However, he claimed that the sex they had in the alley was consensual.

As to the second incident, the defendant denied being involved at all, claiming the second victim was mistaken when she identified him as the perpetrator. The defense also argued that the DNA found at that crime scene was not his. His attorney contended that the DNA at the second crime scene had been contaminated in the Medical Examiner's Office testing laboratory by contact with the defendant's DNA found at the first crime scene.

In addition to the usual jury instructions in this type of case, I instructed the jury that they were to carefully consider the evidence concerning the identification of the defendant. This evidence included the testimony of a defense expert witness, a psychologist, who testified with respect to the second case concerning factors that might tend to influence a witness to make a mistaken identification, such as the perpetrator being of a different race than the victim, who in this case was White.

I also instructed the jury that if they found that the defendant was correctly identified in either case, that factor, standing alone, should not result in a conclusion that the defendant had been correctly identified in the second case or that he was guilty in the second case based on their finding that the defendant had a general propensity to commit this type of crime. However, I also instructed the jury, based on appellate court precedent, that if they found the facts of the two cases sufficiently similar and unique, they could, if they wished, reach a conclusion based on all the evidence in the case that the same person was involved in both incidents.

The jury acquitted the defendant of all charges involving the first victim, apparently finding a reasonable doubt as to whether the first victim did not consent. However, the defendant was convicted of all charges involving the acts in the second incident.

Based on his criminal record of felony convictions in Ohio, the defendant was subject to a life sentence on the second set of charges, which I imposed with a provision that the defendant serve a minimum of 37 years before being eligible for parole. Despite his acquittal in the first case where he claimed this pregnant woman consented to having sex in an alley, I believed the defendant was a dangerous "serial rapist" from whom society needed to be protected. In his own words, he was, indeed, "the devil."

THE JURY SAW NO REASON TO CONVICT

People v. Santos Quinto (12626/07)

The defendant, a man in his 60's at the time of the alleged crimes, was charged with having sexual relations with the then 14-year-old granddaughter of his girlfriend. When the girl, who had come from Ecuador when she was 12 to stay with her grandmother, became pregnant, according to the girl's testimony, her grandmother told her to tell the police that she had been raped by a boy at her school and not to say her grandmother's boyfriend did it.

That boy, also age 14, was arrested, and the girl subsequently had an abortion. But after the police arrested the boy and investigated the girl's story, the girl recanted her accusation, and the charges against the boy were dropped. The police conducted no further investigation into to how the girl became pregnant.

About five years later, the girl, now 19, had moved out of the house and reported to the police that her pregnancy years before had, in fact, been caused by the defendant. At first, she told the police and the District Attorney's Office that the incident happened three years before when she was 16, but when the abortion records were obtained from Planned Parenthood showed she was 14, the girl changed her account about when it happened.

The girl explained that she delayed five years before reporting the true version until she and her younger sister were old enough to move out of the house and away from the defendant. Because the girl was 14 years-old when this happened, the five-year statute of limitations for bringing these felony charges did not begin to run until she turned 18.

At the time of the trial, the grandmother was still living with the defendant and was not called as a witness to support the girl's testimony that she originally told her grandmother that it was the defendant who had made her pregnant.

As is typical of these cases where the victim is young and then delays many years before reporting the sexual assault, the victim's recollection of specific details is vague and incomplete. Often, there are differences in the victim's version each time the victim is asked about what happened.

When the girl had her abortion, according to the medical records, she was spoken to in private by social workers to determine if there was any sexual abuse taking place in the home. The records noted no complaints or evidence of this.

The defense contended the girl's testimony could not be trusted, that she had a long-term dislike of her grandmother and the defendant, and that she was seeking revenge by this false and belated accusation. The defendant, who appeared to be no threat to do this again to anyone, was acquitted.

RAPING RUSSIAN WOMEN IN CONEY ISLAND

People v. Quanel Miller (8048/00)

In 2003, a 65 year-old Russian immigrant living in a Coney Island apartment was returning home from shopping when she was followed into the lobby by a young man who pushed into her apartment after she unlocked the door. The man raped her and took money from her pocketbook. The police were called, but no one could be identified. A sexual assault examination was done at a hospital which resulted in finding DNA from an unknown person, but because it did not match the "DNA profile" of any known person in the nation's various DNA data banks, the person could not be identified.

A person's "DNA profile" is a set of numbers corresponding to the unique DNA characteristics of each person (or that person's identical twin) which are inherited from that person's parents.

Three years later, in 2006, another Russian immigrant living in Coney Island was raped and robbed in her apartment by a man who forced his way in the apartment door. The woman fought back and hit the man with an open paint can resulting in some paint getting on the man's clothes. Among the items stolen were foreign-made cigarettes which were extra-long and wrapped in brown paper. The man lit one of the cigarettes while in the apartment.

When the police were called, they followed a trail of paint drops down the staircase and found a partially smoked cigarette of this type with traces of paint matching the paint thrown in the apartment. DNA was recovered from the cigarette. DNA was also recovered from the second victim during a hospital sexual assault examination. The DNA from the 2006 case matched the DNA profile of the DNA recovered from the 2003 Coney Island rape case, but the person who belonged to that DNA was still unknown.

In 2008, the defendant was arrested for a sexual assault in the Bronx. He had never been arrested before. Pursuant to a court order in that case, a DNA sample was taken from the defendant for use as evidence in the Bronx case. When the DNA profile from the defendant's Bronx case was put into a data bank of DNA profiles, it was found to match the profiles from the 2003 and 2006 Brooklyn rape cases. BINGO!

The victim in the 2003 rape case was unable to identify the defendant as her assailant. The victim in the 2006 case was able to pick the defendant out of a lineup. Both cases were tried together. I denied the defense request for separate trials, because the details of the second crime were so similar to the details of the first crime, that evidence of his committing the second crime in 2006 tended to show he was the person who committed the 2003 crime. Therefore, evidence of the second crime would have been admissible at the trial of the first crime, even if the first crime was tried separately.

The defendant was convicted in both cases of rape, burglary, and robbery. The police investigations at the scenes of each crime and the hospital examinations of both victims that resulted in the recovery of the defendant's DNA were textbook examples of how this type of evidence should be collected and preserved. The defendant's arrest in an unrelated case years later in the Bronx allowed the evidence recovered in the earlier Brooklyn cases to catch up to him.

THE SPRAY MAN AND THE HASIDIC CHILD

People v. Jose Lasanta (9536/10)

The defendant was working as an exterminator. He was accused by a seven year-old Hasidic girl who lived in an apartment he was assigned to work in that while in the apartment he pushed her to a staircase outside the apartment, put his penis in her mouth, and rubbed his penis over her clothing on her breasts.

A cleaning lady was in the apartment at the time. She testified she did not hear anything unusual while the exterminator was there, but she did see the girl crying after the exterminator had left. She had seen the girl sign the exterminator's work sheet when the exterminator arrived. The girl did not tell the cleaning lady why she was crying.

The girl's mother testified she saw the defendant arrive in the lobby on her way out of the building and told him he did not have to do any work in her apartment, although she did sign his work sheet. When she came back to the apartment hours later, her daughter was already speaking about the incident with her father. She did not want her daughter to see a doctor, "because it would endanger her emotional stability."

The child's father testified he was in the basement of the building when his daughter came down crying and told him what "the spray man" had done. He looked out on the street but did not see the defendant's vehicle. He did not notify the police until the next day, because he wanted to consult first with his rabbi in Israel about what to do. He denied having any intention of suing the exterminating company or the landlord who hired the company for what had happened.

The defendant testified and said that he had been in the apartment to do his work and that nothing happened. He denied being told by the child's mother not to go into the apartment. He said that after he left the apartment, he went to two other apartments in the building but no one answered the doors there. He then went to the building next door and left his vehicle on the street until he completed his work there.

This evidence was intended to show that the defendant remained at the scene after supposedly attacking the girl which, if true, would be inconsistent with his having committed the attack and rebut the father's testimony that he looked for the defendant shortly after his daughter told him what happened.

During her testimony, the child was asked by the defense to describe the color of the exterminator's penis. The prosecution objected, but I allowed the question. The girl said she could not remember. When the defendant later testified, he said he had a "brown" penis, but the defense did not offer a photograph or other testimony about its color, and the prosecution did not request to see it.

The girl was eight years-old when she testified and could not recall several details about what happened. Her apparent lack of recollection may have been caused by a reluctance to speak about the matter, but it affected her believability as a witness. Her trial testimony also differed slightly from what she had told the police and the grand jury when she testified there.

It is difficult for an adult victim to testify about a sexual assault, and where the victim is a child from a religious household, it is even more difficult. Often these cases come down to how much the jury is willing take these difficulties into consideration and believe the witness despite the flaws in the testimony.

The defendant was previously convicted of manslaughter for shooting and killing someone after an argument on the street 21 years before this incident, which the jury learned about when he testified. I instructed the jury that this conviction could be considered only on the issue of whether it would affect their evaluation of the defendant's credibility as a witness and must not be considered as evidence that the defendant had a criminal propensity.

The defense argued that the parents' delay in reporting the incident to the police was because the parents initially did not believe it happened. That argument may have been enough to tip the scales in favor of a reasonable doubt. The defendant was found not guilty even though there was no reason offered as to why the girl would make this all up other than, according to the defense summation, "the girl felt neglected and was looking for attention."

CAUGHT IN THE ACT OF DOING NOTHING WRONG

People v. Arturo Saldana (6596/09)

Where charges of rape and assault take place in the context of domestic violence, juries often must put themselves in the shoes of the alleged victim to appreciate the circumstances of the case. Where jurors tell themselves they would have behaved differently, they often, without even realizing they are doing this, "blame the victim" and then find that the victim's story is not believable. This case may be an example.

The victim and the defendant had a 10-year relationship, beginning when she was 13 and he was 18. They had one child together. When the victim was pregnant by the defendant with their second child, she came to believe that the defendant was having an affair. Although the defendant denied this to her, she made the defendant leave their third floor apartment which was in a three-family house in which her parents lived in the first floor apartment.

Although the defendant no longer lived in the house, he maintained a relationship with his two children who continued to live in the house with the victim. The victim testified that she was no longer romantically involved with the defendant, but on cross-examination she admitted that a year after she broke up with the defendant, she had taken a trip to Maryland to visit his parents with whom the defendant was then staying. While there, she also admitted that she slept in the same bedroom with him, but she claimed it was not in the same bed.

The alleged crime occurred about two months after this trip. The victim said the defendant came to her house in an attempt to reconcile but she was not willing to do this. The victim said the defendant became angry and said he believed the victim was now seeing another man. He then took her cell phone and broke it before leaving.

After going to bed that night with the younger child in her bed and the older child sleeping with her parents on the first floor, the victim said she awoke early the next morning at about 6:00 am to find the defendant straddling her in bed.

She said she attempted to fight him off, but he continued to punch her in the face and throat until she lost consciousness. While hitting her, the victim testified the defendant said, "It was hard for me to get in the window."

She said she regained consciousness when she heard her father's voice in the house. When she awoke, the defendant was on top of her without his shirt on, her nightgown was raised to her chest, and her panties were off. She testified she was unable to speak due to the pain in her face and throat from being punched.

At this point, her parents came into the room. Her mother asked the defendant what he had done, and he answered he had not done anything. He then walked down the stairs to leave the house, but was met and arrested by the police who were responding to a 911call made by the father.

Another aspect of domestic violence cases is the knowledge that each party has of the prior misdeeds of the other party. Thus, on cross-examination, defense counsel was able to ask the victim about various gangs she had belonged to when she was younger and the physical altercations she had with other women during the five years preceding this incident. The victim was also asked about threats of physical violence she had made to the woman she believed the defendant was having an affair with. She admitted to not telling the prosecutor about the trip she had made to Maryland and sleeping in the same room with the defendant until after the prosecutor showed her a video of her at the defendant's mother's home, which defense counsel had provided to the prosecutor's office.

A hospital examination of the victim showed no evidence of vaginal trauma. Ambulance records did not reflect that the victim was bleeding, although she was bruised about the face. Evidence obtained from the hospital examination was tested at the Medical Examiner's Office and revealed the defendant's DNA was present on a vaginal swab taken from the victim.

The defense called the boyfriend of the defendant's sister who did repair work at the victim's house after the defendant had moved out. He testified that during this period he saw the defendant there frequently in the company of the victim.

The defendant's sister also testified. She said she had become friends with the victim during the 10 years the victim was with her brother. She saw the defendant at the victim's house on several occasions after he purportedly was thrown out by the victim.

The defendant's 12-year-old niece testified that the victim and the defendant accompanied her and several others to Coney Island on her birthday which was four days before the incident. The defense also called the woman with whom the victim testified she believed the defendant was having an affair with while he was living with the victim. This woman testified that at that time the victim had attacked her in a bar with a Snapple bottle and that she had told the victim that she had broken off her relationship with the defendant.

To refute the claim that the defendant had somehow gotten into the victim's apartment through a window, the defense called the tenant who lived on the second floor of the house. He testified that due to repairs being made, there were no locks on the front door at the time of the incident.

Finally, the defendant, with no criminal record, testified he had consensual sex with the victim that day and did not hit her. In fact, on several occasions when they were together, she had hit him and once chased him with a knife. On the date preceding the incident, he was at her house during the day, and the victim said she wanted to go out with him that night. He had plans to go out with a friend, and she became angry when he told her this. He came back to the victim's apartment early the next morning. He testified the victim was awake, and, after he brushed his teeth, they had consensual sexual intercourse.

According to the defendant, the victim then accused him of mistakenly calling her by his former girlfriend's name, and she became angry. She said if you are going with her, then give me full custody of the kids. He refused. She then got up from the bed and fell injuring herself. Her father came upstairs and saw him patting the victim's injured cheeks and forehead with a wet cloth.

Although the defendant's testimony may have been contrived to meet the incriminating details in the case, the victim's behavior before and after the incident probably was not the type of behavior that most jurors could personally relate to. The defendant did not appear to be a threat to anyone, and the victim had physically recovered from whatever injuries the defendant may have inflicted. He was found not guilty of all charges

DNA SOLVES THE CASE AND A JUROR'S MISCONDUCT

People v. Anthony Jameson (8042/06)

In this rape case, the defendant was arrested 10 years after the crime following a match of DNA taken from the victim in this case with DNA taken from the defendant in North Carolina following his convictions in that state for several felonies.

There is a national data base of DNA profiles of persons convicted of crimes throughout the country. Many states, including New York, require that defendants convicted of crimes provide a DNA sample (usually from a skin cell swab taken from inside their cheek) that goes into this data base. In many ways, this system resembles the data base of fingerprints that have been kept for decades by individual states and the F.B.I. This case is an example of how the DNA data base system works.

This case is also an example of how misconduct by a juror discovered after the verdict almost resulted in having the conviction set aside and a new trial ordered.

The victim, a 20 year-old young lady at the time, was walking home at night from the subway after working at her job as a clothing store manager. As she was passing a park, she was forced into the park by three teenage males, one of whom held a hard object to her back and told her she would be shot if she did not do what they said. Two of the males went through her pocketbook and took money and also took her ring and a bracelet while the third male raped her and then slashed her face leaving a scar from her ear to her mouth.

After looking at files of photographs of males with prior arrests, the victim identified a photograph of someone she believed was the rapist and then picked that person out of a lineup. However, that person's DNA did not match the DNA in semen recovered in a vaginal swab taken at the hospital from the victim. Ten years later, the DNA profile from that swab was compared to profiles in a national data base and found to match the defendant's DNA profile that was also in that data base.

After discussing with the attorneys how not to reveal to the jury that it was the defendant's convictions in North Carolina that resulted in his DNA being in the data base, it was agreed that I could tell the jury, that the national data base has DNA profiles of many people for various reasons, and the jury should not speculate as to why the defendant's DNA profile was included in that data base. The investigating detective testified that he was notified that there was a match of the DNA taken from the victim in this case with the defendant's profile that was in the data base. Following notification, the detective testified he located the defendant in Georgia.

After locating the defendant, the detective arrested the defendant and the defendant was brought to New York where, pursuant to a court order, a DNA sample was taken from the defendant's cheek cell with an oral swab.

Technicians from the Medical Examiner's Office testified to the scientific procedures involved in obtaining DNA profiles from the hospital swab taken from the victim and the oral swab taken from the defendant and that the two profiles matched and established to odds of greater than one in a trillion that the two samples came from different people.

The victim could not identify the defendant after so much time had passed. The jury also heard testimony that she had originally identified someone else as the rapist whose DNA did not match the DNA taken from her at the hospital. Nevertheless, the DNA evidence against the defendant was strong circumstantial evidence of his guilt.

Faced with this evidence, the defendant chose to testify. He admitted having sex with the victim but under entirely different circumstances. Because the defendant's believability as a witness was an issue for the jury, I allowed the jury to hear that he had been convicted of four felonies in North Carolina, which his own lawyer brought out from the defendant before the prosecution had a chance to do it on cross-examination.

The defendant testified that at the time of the crime, he was a member of the Bloods gang and on the day before the reported date of the incident, he met the complaining witness at a Bloods initiation ceremony for prospective female members when she came to an apartment to have consensual sex with several male Bloods. He testified that, unlike the other males there who had sex with her, he did not use a condom at the time, thereby providing an alternative explanation for how his DNA was found in her vagina the next day.

According to his testimony, he had no contact with the victim the next day and was not in the park when the reported rape, robbery, and face slashing took place.

In rebuttal, the prosecution called the victim's cousin who testified she knew the victim her whole life and that the victim was never in a gang. This witness also corroborated that at the time of the crime the victim was a manger in a clothing store, had a steady boyfriend, and never knew the victim to have expressed any interest in becoming a gang member.

The jury convicted the defendant of all charges.

The day after the verdict and prior to sentencing, I received a letter about the case from an attorney that had been hand delivered to the Clerk's Office. The letter said the writer had been out to dinner with a group of six other women, three of whom she did not previously know. During that dinner, she heard one of the women she did not previously know, but whose name she provided in the letter, say she was currently a juror on a rape case in Brooklyn. This woman told the group at the dinner that the case "involved gangs" and that her "mind was made up about guilt," although she knew she "had a duty to deliberate." The juror also said she had "Googled" the defense attorney and found out that he was in private practice and that "the case involved DNA" and the defendant had testified the sex was consensual.

The writer of the letter also said that during the dinner the juror had learned she was an attorney and privately asked her opinion about the case, but the writer told the juror she could not talk to her about the case. Indeed, what the juror was doing in seeking to discuss the case was wrong and in violation of my instructions given daily throughout the trial not to discuss the case with anyone and keep an open mind about the case until deliberations at the end of the case. As an attorney, the letter writer immediately knew that the juror was violating the basic instructions given to jurors in every case.

What I found particularly disappointing was that the letter writer was an appellate attorney for an organization that handled criminal appeals for indigent defendants, so she should have been familiar with the basic administrative operations of the Brooklyn Supreme Court. In explaining why she delayed for a few days before notifying the court about what happened, the writer stated that she did not know how to determine the particular courtroom where this case was being tried and, therefore, she waited to consult a supervisor in her organization. A simple telephone call to the Clerks' Office or to the chambers of the Administrative Judge describing the case and describing the problem would have enabled her to obtain this information, which is eventually what was done.

I had my suspicions that the letter writer delayed reporting the incident, because she was waiting to see if there would be a conviction. If there had been an acquittal, the letter writer would not have had to do anything, and the juror would not have gotten into any trouble. If this information had come to my attention before the jury had begun deliberating on the case, this juror would have been excused for misconduct and an alternate juror substituted.

I turned the letter over to the attorneys and, as expected, the defendant's attorney made a motion to set aside the verdict based on juror misconduct that prejudiced the defendant. I ordered a hearing, and the letter writer testified to what she heard the juror say.

The juror also testified at this hearing. She testified she did not recall speaking about the case at the dinner. She said she had some wine during dinner which may have affected her memory. She testified that she had not made up her mind about the case until deliberations had begun, that she listened to the opinions of other jurors, and that she did not share with the other jurors what she had learned about the defense attorney on the Internet.

At the conclusion of the hearing, I found that although the juror had violated my instructions not to discuss the case, what the juror had said and done did not prejudice the defendant and there was no evidence that anyone at the dinner offered any opinions on the case that may have influenced the juror.

The motion to set aside the verdict was denied.

I did not mention one important fact about the case. At the time of the crime, the defendant was 15-years-old. In New York, the age of full criminal responsibility is 16, which is younger than many other states where the age is 17 or 18. Because the charges here were included in a statute setting forth certain crimes where 15-year-olds can be prosecuted "as adults" rather than treated as juveniles in Family Court, the defendant was eligible for adult treatment.

However, rather than the maximum adult sentence of 25 years for each of his crimes of rape, robbery, and assault, the maximum time he could serve for all of these crimes, due to his age, would be 10 years with a 5 year minimum before being eligible for release on parole, which was the sentence I imposed.

I could have held additional proceedings to determine whether the juror should be held in contempt of court for violating my repeated instructions not to discuss the case. However, I believed the juror was put through enough having to testify at the hearing to set aside the verdict. She did apologize for violating my instructions during her testimony, and I believed she was terribly embarrassed and truly sorry.

A DEFENDANT'S BIZARRE DNA EXPLANATION

People v. Frank Ryer (12335/07)

This is yet another case of rape where a defendant who is connected to the crime by DNA evidence came up with a creative, but ultimately unconvincing explanation. The case involved an unfortunate family situation where the defendant raped his 12-year-old stepdaughter. The mother of the 12-year-old rape victim who was the wife of the defendant was in prison at the time.

The victim and her seven-year-old half-brother, the son of the defendant, were living with their grandmother, the mother of the imprisoned woman. The young girl did not report the rape to anyone until six months later when the grandmother noticed the girl appeared to be pregnant.

According to the testimony of the young girl, the defendant came to the grandmother's home to see his son. The defendant, while the grandmother was in another room, came into the girl's bedroom and forcibly had sexual intercourse with her on her bed. She said this was the first time she had intercourse and was embarrassed and afraid to tell anyone what happened.

A psychologist testified for the prosecution to explain to the jury that such a reaction is not uncommon and is known as the "rape trauma syndrome." As I instructed the jury, the psychologist would not be allowed to give an opinion whether the girl in this case had actually been raped, because that would be a decision solely for the jury to make. I further explained that the psychologist was testifying about this syndrome, because the jury might otherwise believe that every child would immediately tell an adult about being raped.

The child's grandmother testified that about six months after the incident, she noticed that the child appeared to be pregnant. The child was taken to a doctor who confirmed the pregnancy with a blood test. The grandmother then notified the police and the defendant was arrested.

In this case, the DNA evidence incriminating the defendant did not come from physical evidence the rapist left on the victim. Rather, when the child gave birth to a boy three months later, DNA samples were taken from the baby and compared with DNA samples taken from the baby's mother and from the defendant. Analysis of the samples by the Medical Examiner's Office established a greater than 99.99% probability that the defendant was the father of that baby, thereby confirming the charge that he had intercourse with the victim.

Because the defendant was at least 18 years-old, in fact he was 49 years-old, and the victim was less than 13 years-old, the charge was Rape in the First Degree based on their respective ages. The use or threat of the use of physical force by the defendant was not required to prove this charge.

Faced with this evidence, the defendant, in an effort to discredit the DNA results, called as an expert witness a doctor of osteopathy who had no personal experience in DNA testing. Instead, this witness testified that DNA samples require special handling to preserve their characteristics against contamination and degradation by outside elements and that the procedures he followed in his office for submitting DNA samples were more stringent than the procedures employed when the samples in this case were taken from the defendant and the victim.

Now for the defendant's explanation: He testified that he was married to the child's mother and was the father of the seven-year-old boy. He also testified that before he married the victim's mother, he had a child by that woman who was, in fact, the victim in this case, even though his name was not on her birth certificate.

According to this explanation, he was actually the grandfather of the baby delivered by the victim and the actual father was someone else, who the victim was concealing. This explanation, according to the defendant, would account for why the DNA testing showed he was related to the baby, but as the baby's grandfather, not the father.

In rebuttal, the prosecution called other witnesses from the Medical Examiner's Office to explain that there was no evidence that the DNA samples in this case were contaminated or degraded which would have been apparent from the testing if that had happened.

These witnesses also testified that the DNA analysis showed the defendant was not the victim's father as he had claimed, because his DNA had certain characteristics that were not present in the victim's DNA which he would have passed down to her if he were actually her father. Based on this analysis, it was scientifically impossible for the defendant to be the victim's father as he had claimed in his testimony.

The defendant was convicted, leaving the grandmother to take care of three children whose parents were in prison: the victim; the victim's brother; and the victim's baby, and leaving the victim with a very sad story to tell her baby when he got older concerning the identity of his father.

Chapter 12. *BURGLARY AND ROBBERY TRIALS*

HE MAY HAVE BEEN DRUNK, BUT NOT DRUNK ENOUGH
People v. Anthony Boyd (2257/11)

Under the law, a "burglary" consists of knowingly and unlawfully entering or remaining in a building with an intent to commit a crime inside the building. Where the building is a dwelling (defined as a building usually occupied by a person for overnight lodging), the crime is a higher degree of burglary. Burglary is a separate crime from any crime that may be committed inside, such as stealing property, which is a larceny, or forcibly stealing property from another person, which is a robbery, or damaging property inside, which is known as "criminal mischief." This case is an example of the need to prove all of the parts of the definition of burglary in order to convict of that crime.

In this trial, a tenant in a third floor apartment testified to observing the defendant on his fire escape putting his head through an open bathroom window at about 7:00 am. The defendant said to the tenant, "The crackers set me up. I just want to get to the street." The tenant smelled alcohol on the defendant's breath, and the defendant appeared to be either intoxicated or high on drugs. The police were called and they found a hat on the roof which was later tested and found to contain the defendant's DNA.

The defendant went down the fire escape. A short time later in a nearby building, the female owner of the four-story building was awakened by noises coming from an unoccupied top floor apartment. She testified she had a handgun in her apartment that had belonged to her deceased father. She took the gun into the hallway and saw the defendant. She told him to get out and followed him down the stairs. The defendant appeared intoxicated to her, and he had difficulty opening the door to the street. When the defendant turned towards her, she started shooting at him. She did not report this incident to the police.

The defendant was shot once in the back and went to a hospital. He told the hospital staff that he had been shot in a park over an argument concerning a cigarette. The hospital staff reported the bullet wound to the police as required by law. The police spoke with the defendant at the hospital and then went to the park but found no ballistic evidence, such as bullets or spent shell casings, to indicate that a shooting had taken place.

A police review of 911 calls that morning disclosed that someone had reported a shooting in the vicinity of the woman's building. The police went there and saw a parked car with its windows shot out and two shell casings on the street directly across from the front door of the woman's building.

The woman answered the police knock on her door and initially denied knowing anything about a shooting that morning. However, upon further questioning, she quickly broke down and told the police that she had fired the shots at an intruder. She was not prosecuted for either the shooting or the possession of the gun and agreed to testify as a witness in the case.

At the trial in which the defendant was charged with a burglary of each building, the defendant's attorney argued that the defendant was so intoxicated that he was incapable of forming an intent to commit a crime in either building. Therefore, he was only guilty, at most, of trespassing in both buildings, which is a misdemeanor.

The defendant was found guilty of attempting to trespass in the first building. The jury apparently found that he did not "enter" that building even though the witness said he put his head through the open window. Instead, the jury found he was in the act of trying to enter it through the open window. The jury apparently also had a reasonable doubt that the defendant had an "intent to commit a crime" inside, perhaps giving some credence to his statement that he just was trying to get to the street.

As to the second building, the defendant was convicted of burglary even though there was no evidence that he committed any crimes inside the building. His being shot in the back by the owner of the building did not generate enough sympathy for him for the jury to have acquitted him of that charge. Compare this situation to the facts of the Derek Williams case, discussed below, where the defendant was also shot by the occupant during the crime.

Burglary of a dwelling is classified as a "violent felony offense" even if the defendant did not engage in violence. Because the defendant had two prior felony convictions that were also classified as "violent felony offenses," he was required to be found a "persistent violent felony offender," which mandated that a life sentence be imposed.

A SON'S REVENGE GOES TOO FAR FOR THE JURY

People v. Derek Williams (6458/11)

Juries will acquit even though the evidence would support a conviction where there is something about the case that they don't like, especially where they have no sympathy for the victim or they believe the victim's testimony was not entirely truthful. This was such a case.

The victims in this case lived in a house where the mother ran several "Susu's," which are a form of savings accounts where

112

participants contribute every week and periodically one of the participants gets to withdraw all the money. At the time of this incident, the mother had, according to her, about $25,000 in her home. The defendant came to the door saying he had a deposit to make. When the door was opened, he pushed himself in at gunpoint and demanded the Susu money in the house from the mother and her daughter. A co-defendant who pled guilty prior to trial then entered the house and started looking for the money.

In cases such as this where juries hear that other people are arrested, they are told not to speculate why the case against the other person was separated from the defendant's case, so this jury did not know that the other person had pled guilty. Otherwise, there is a risk that a jury will infer that because a co-defendant pled guilty, that, in itself, is some proof that a crime actually was committed and the defendant on trial was a participant.

The co-defendant, after not finding money on the first floor, then went upstairs and encountered a son in his 20's who lived in the home. According to the son, he struggled with the co-defendant and obtained the gun from him. His testimony about this was challenged on cross-examination, with the implication that, in fact, the son had his own gun and the co-defendant was unarmed. The son went downstairs with the gun and shot at the defendant, striking him 3 or 4 times. The co-defendant also came downstairs and ran out of the house.

The son pursued the co-defendant in his car, eventually catching up to him and striking him with the car. As the co-defendant was lying in the street, the son beat him with his hands and a garbage can cover until the co-defendant was motionless. In return for his testimony, the son was given immunity from prosecution for shooting the defendant and this beating of the co-defendant.

When the mother and daughter in the house originally reported the incident to the police, they never mentioned that the son was even present. At trial, the mother and daughter claimed not to have been in the room when the son shot the defendant, even though the son testified his mother and sister were there.

The prosecution took the rather implausible position that the mother and daughter were telling the truth about not seeing the son shoot the defendant, rather than conceding that they were initially trying to avoid getting the son into trouble for shooting the defendant and beating up the co-defendant.

The defense argued that none of the prosecution witnesses could be trusted and that the story about an attempt to rob Sussu money could have been made up to excuse the son's actions for his unjustified shooting, his illegal possession of a gun, and his assault on the co-defendant. Because the defendant was the one who was shot, and because it appeared that the purported victims were unhurt and had not had anything actually taken from them, as well as apparently not telling the whole truth about what happened, there was room for the jury to find reasonable doubt. The defendant was acquitted of all charges. The fact that the co-defendant had pled guilty to an attempted robbery in this case was not considered by the jury, because, as noted, under the law the jury could not be told about this.

HE WAS EITHER A BURGLAR OR A LOVER

People v. Sadiq Abdul-Wahaab (1319/11)

The victim came home to his apartment just before noon to find three men inside, two wearing bandanas around their faces and a third wearing a hockey goalie mask. The apartment door lock had been broken open and the glass french doors to one of the bedrooms had its glass broken. The defendant was allegedly the person wearing the hockey mask. Although he had grown up across the street and the victim knew him from the neighborhood, the victim did not recognize his face under the hockey mask.

The defendant pointed a gun at the victim and ordered him to step aside as all three men left the apartment. The victim's father, who also lived in the apartment, was a bishop in a local church and was conducting Sunday mass at the time. Perhaps this is why no one from the household was expected to be home that morning.

After the thieves left, the victim called 911. Shortly after, the police arrived, the defendant came over to the apartment to ask the victim if he was alright, which certainly was inconsistent with his being a perpetrator. They spoke briefly and, thereafter, the defendant was not seen in the neighborhood, which, on the other hand, was consistent with him being a perpetrator.

Police investigators came to the apartment to try to see if fingerprints of the perpetrators could be obtained but were not successful. After the police left, family members were cleaning the ransacked apartment. A cousin found a bloody tissue in the bedroom under a pile of clothing. The police came back to the apartment and were given the tissue. It was found to have the defendant's DNA on it, which already was in a data bank due to his prior convictions. This was the main evidence against the defendant.

At trial, the defendant called the victim's sister as a witness. She also lived in the apartment. Defense counsel asked her about her having a sexual relationship the defendant, which she vehemently denied.

The defendant then testified. He denied committing the burglary and claimed that the day before the burglary he had sex with the victim's sister in the bedroom. He claimed that when he was there, the glass door in the bedroom broke and he cut himself trying to repair it. He testified he used a tissue to stop the bleeding and then left the tissue in the bedroom.

The jury convicted the defendant, not believing that he had a sexual relationship with the bishop's daughter as an explanation for how his blood was found on the tissue in the bedroom.

A CARJACKING FOR A BAG OF CELL PHONES

People v. Ernest Bennt and Jason Daniels (3966/10)

In this robbery case where the two defendants were apparently caught in the act by the police, the defendants had a different version of what happened.

The victim was in the business of selling cell phones to stores and individuals. He kept the cell phones in his car. After leaving a store where he had sold some phones for re-sale, the victim testified he was attacked and thrown into his car by the defendants. One of the defendants drove the car with the victim seated inside it to another location. The victim was held in the car while the other defendant, who had followed in a second car, started taking cell phones from the victim's car and putting them into his car. The first defendant, while still in the victim's car, demanded the victim's wallet and pulled off the victim's pants.

Two witnesses to the carjacking had called 911 and described the victim's car. This information was relayed to police in the neighborhood, including two plainclothes officers, who saw the victim's car parked at the second location. Although the eyewitnesses who made the telephone calls did not testify at the trial, recordings of their 911 calls were played for the jury.

The rules of evidence permitted this, because these calls qualified as a "present sense impression." The callers were obviously describing something that they were seeing as the event was taking place and another witness, the victim, corroborated the details of the events described in the telephone calls. These details included the make and color of the victim's car and a physical description of the two perpetrators which matched the defendants' descriptions.

The two plainclothes police officers testified that when they approached the victim's car with their guns drawn and identified themselves as police, the second defendant, who was loading the cell phones into his car, ran as did the first defendant who had been inside the victim's car. The two officers gave chase, and about three blocks away they apprehended the defendants trying to hide in a doorway. The police also observed the victim exit his car in his underwear and bleeding from his face.

One of the defendants, who had no prior criminal record, testified and claimed that there was never a carjacking. He testified he had made previous arrangements with the victim to buy 30 Blackberry brand cell phones for $1500. He gave the victim $1500 and the victim gave him a plastic garbage bag containing

Blackberry boxes which he assumed contained the cell phones he had paid for. Before the victim could drive away, this defendant testified he discovered that the boxes did not contain Blackberry brand phones, and the other defendant, who was his cousin, reached into the driver's window and grabbed the victim to stop him from driving off with their money. When the defendant saw the two plainclothes officers approaching with their guns drawn, he did not know they were police so he and his cousin ran from them.

The jury convicted both defendants of robbery. The 911 calls describing the victim being pushed into his car at the first location was, doubtless, a strong factor in the jury's believing the victim's version of the events.

HE SHOULD HAVE ORDERED FRIES WITH THAT
People v. Neb Morrow (9552/09)

In this trial involving an armed robbery of a McDonald's, the defendant chose to represent himself. Under the law, a defendant has a constitutional right to waive his right to be represented by an attorney as long the court warns the defendant of the risks involved in self-representation and the defendant understands these risks. The trial judge is required in engage the defendant in a discussion to explain that although the defendant may not be an attorney, the defendant will be required to follow the rules and procedures involved in a trial and that the court is not required to instruct the defendant what should be done during the trial or how to do it.

Interestingly, a defendant seeking to represent himself is not required to know the rules and procedures involved in a trial, but only to be aware of the risks involved in self-representation. As long as a defendant is aware of the risks, makes a "timely request," to represent himself so that the trial is not delayed by this request, and the defendant demonstrates that he will follow the rulings of the court and not be disruptive, a court must grant this request.

A wrongfully denied request for self-representation will result in a reversal of a conviction on appeal, even if the lawyer representing the defendant who wanted to represent himself did an excellent job.

Where a request for self-representation is granted, courts often appoint "stand-by" counsel, to sit in the courtroom and follow the proceedings in order to be available to step in and represent the defendant should the defendant change his mind during the trial about wanting to represent himself. What is not allowed is "hybrid representation" where a defendant wishes to represent himself for certain parts of the trial and have a lawyer represent him for the other parts of the trial.

Some courts allow the stand-by attorney to sit at the defense table with the defendant and be available as a "legal advisor" to answer the defendant's questions during the trial. Other courts, as I do, take the position that the stand-by attorney does not represent the defendant until such time as the defendant no longer wishes to represent himself, and, therefore, the stand-by attorney will not be available to consult with the defendant during the trial.

The reason I take this approach is that if the stand-by attorney has a whispered conversation with the defendant during the trial and the defendant then goes ahead and does something that hurts his case, the trial record will not show whether the defendant did this based on bad advice received from the stand-by attorney or, instead, chose to ignore different advice and made the blunder on his own.

Where an attorney's blunder is sufficiently significant, an appellate court may reverse a conviction based on a violation of the defendant's Sixth Amendment constitutional right to the "effective assistance of counsel." That right, of course, does not apply to a blunder made by a defendant who is representing himself. Not allowing a stand-by attorney to silently advise a defendant during a trial avoids the potential of a defendant blaming his own mistakes on advice he never received in an effort to vacate a trial conviction.

A second reason for my not allowing the stand-by attorney to advise the defendant during the trial is that once I explain to a defendant seeking to represent himself that he will be sitting alone at his table and will not have an attorney available to give him advice during a trial, that defendant may decide not to represent himself. To me, this is a much better choice, because the trial will run more smoothly, and the defendant will actually receive competent legal representation.

In my discussions with defendants who wish to represent themselves, in order to explain the risks involved, I often note the adage that, "a lawyer who chooses to represent himself has a fool for a client," meaning that even someone with legal training is better off being represented by an attorney. I even tell defendants during these discussions that although a defendant seeking to represent himself may believe that a jury seeing a defendant representing himself will feel admiration for his courage and sincerity, it is more likely that the jury will simply believe that the defendant representing himself is emotionally unstable and, therefore, dangerous.

Despite my detailed warnings to this defendant of the risks involved in representing himself, he chose to go that route. This was no surprise to me, because only months before, this same defendant had unsuccessfully represented himself in a federal court trial where he was charged with robbing two Radio Shack stores in Queens. He, therefore, was well-aware of the risks involved in representing himself. But, because he had demonstrated that he would follow the rulings of the court during that trial, I really had no alternative other than to grant his request to again be his own lawyer.

The robbery in this case was depicted in a surveillance video taken inside the store. It showed the robber displaying a gun wearing a hooded sweatshirt so his face was not visible. The robber demanded that an employee give him the cash from two registers. The cash was put in a McDonald's paper bag which the robber put in a leather messenger bag carried on a shoulder strap. None of the several employees in the store was able to get a good look at the face of the robber, but his clothing and messenger bag were described.

As the robber left the store, several 911 calls were made by employees, and two employees followed the robber down 4th Avenue, a busy commercial street. The robber was seen trying to hail a cab and then pass the entrance of a subway station.

The two employees saw the police join their foot pursuit in a car which contained a third store employee. The two employees on the street saw the police capture the defendant. They each testified the police captured the same man they had followed from the store. The defendant was captured after he was ordered at gunpoint by the police to drop to the ground. In doing so, according to the police, the defendant dropped the messenger bag he had been carrying which contained a loaded gun and a McDonald's paper bag containing $1526.58, the exact amount taken from the registers.

The store employees identified the messenger bag, and the jury could see the messenger bag for themselves in court and compare it to the bag seen being carried by the robber on the surveillance video. The jury was also able to view a photograph of the defendant taken after his arrest showing him wearing a hooded sweatshirt and compare the sweatshirt to the one being worn by the robber as shown on the surveillance video, as well as compare the overall physical appearance of the defendant with the robber as he appeared on that video.

The defendant, who was arrested wearing a gray hooded sweatshirt, claimed he was mistakenly identified and relied on the fact that some witnesses described the hooded sweatshirt the robber was wearing as black. The defendant relied on the fact that the police did not attempt to take fingerprints or DNA samples from either the gun or any of the other property in an effort to establish that the defendant ever touched those items.

The defendant testified. Rather than ask himself questions and then answer them, he was permitted to tell his version of the events in narrative form and then answer the prosecutor's questions on cross-examination. The defendant testified that he sold his own artwork on the street and that he was in the neighborhood after delivering a painting to a customer there, whose name he did not know. The defendant claimed that the police in the local precinct knew him and did not like him, because of disputes there about his selling his artwork on the street.

He testified he was on his way home waiting for a cab when two males ran past him into a subway station, but before doing this, one of them threw the messenger bag under a nearby car. Just as that happened, the police came by and arrested him even though he told the police that what they were looking for was under the car.

The defendant also claimed the police emptied the contents of the messenger bag on the street and that the contents did not fall out of the bag when he dropped the bag as testified to by the police. The defendant also claimed he was wearing a black hooded sweatshirt with a gray lining but the police turned it inside out when his arrest photograph was taken so that the outside of the sweatshirt would then be gray and match the description of the gray sweatshirt that was given by most of the witnesses.

The jury was made aware of the defendant's extensive prior criminal record which included two convictions for gun possession and three convictions for robbery, including the two recent convictions in federal court for the Radio Shack robberies. As to those convictions, the defendant told the jury he had also represented himself at those trials and was convicted there, because the witnesses had lied and that the trial judge in that case knew the witnesses were lying at that trial.

The jury quickly convicted and did not ask any questions during their deliberations nor did they request to view any of the over 20 trial exhibits.   Based on the defendant's prior record for robbery and weapons convictions, I sentenced him to 21 years to life to run consecutively to his federal robbery sentences, meaning that his sentence in this case would not start until he completed the sentence in the federal case.

ALMOST AS EASY AS TAKING CANDY FROM A BABY

People v. William Dixon (7199/08)

The victim in this case was a young Hasidic man pushing his eight month-old baby in a stroller. He was in an alley taking a short cut between two streets when the defendant approached holding a plastic bag and pointed it at the victim as if there was a gun inside the bag. According to the victim, the defendant said, "I have a gun. Give me your stuff." However, perhaps not believing the defendant actually had a gun, the victim grabbed the bag revealing that there was no gun inside.

The defendant then punched the victim and reached into the stroller removing the victim's camera. The punch caused the victim's cell phone to fall out of his pocket. The defendant picked up the phone and fled.

A second man, also an Orthodox Jew, was in the alley and saw what had happened. He briefly chased the defendant but lost sight of him when the defendant ran into a building. The bystander then called 911.

After the police arrived, the bystander was speaking with the police when he saw the defendant approaching from a different direction from the building that he had run into. The prosecution presented diagrams of the neighborhood streets and buildings to show how the defendant could have made his way through the interior of the buildings to have emerged from a building in the opposite direction from where the thief had run.

The bystander pointed out the defendant to the police who grabbed the defendant after a foot chase. The defendant was in possession of the victim's cell phone and camera. The victim identified the defendant on the street while the police had him in custody.

The defendant had five prior felony convictions which involved a residential burglary, a robbery where the victim's chain was snatched, two separate drug sales, and an assault on a court officer in a courtroom during one of his criminal cases. He did not testify at this trial, so the jury was unaware of his criminal record which I had ruled could have been brought out to impeach his credibility as a witness if he testified.

His attorney argued that the defendant was mistakenly identified, and that he simply found the property after the real thief threw it away.

The jury found the defendant not guilty of Robbery in the Second Degree, which required a "display of what appeared to be" a gun by holding a bag which manifested the presence of a gun, and a second charge of Robbery in the Second Degree, which required causing "physical injury" to the victim during a robbery. Apparently, the jury did not believe beyond a reasonable doubt that the hand in the bag sufficiently resembled a gun or that the punch caused the requisite "substantial pain" to the victim. However, the jury did convict the defendant of Robbery in the Third Degree, which required only that property be forcibly taken.

Nevertheless, based on the defendant's record of five prior felony convictions, on at least two of which he served one year or more in prison, I had the discretion to sentence the defendant, as a "persistent felony offender," to life imprisonment with a minimum term of between 15 and 25 years before being eligible for release on parole. Based on the defendant's record and his selection in this case of a particularly vulnerable victim who was pushing a baby in a stroller, I sentenced the defendant to 15 years to life in prison

Chapter 13. *ASSAULT TRIALS*

THE VICTIM DECIDES TO TELL THE POLICE WHO DID IT

People v. Kevin Reaves (1409/09)

The victim was a gang member and a registered sex offender, based on a prior rape conviction, who was recently released from prison after being convicted of assault. He returned to his old neighborhood and went to the "spot" where he used to buy marijuana. He was confronted by a person he identified as the defendant and an argument ensued about whether the victim was a member of the Folk Nation gang. The dispute quieted down, and the victim left thinking the matter was over.

As the victim was walking on Parkside Avenue a few blocks away, the defendant approached wearing a hooded sweatshirt. He pulled the hood off so the victim could see his face and then shot the victim three times. The victim recovered from the injuries but refused to cooperate with the police or give any information about who shot him. As he later testified, the victim was afraid of retaliation. The victim also testified that he planned to take revenge for the shooting himself and did not want to involve the police.

Several months later, the victim was in the local police station on a matter relating to his registration there as a sex offender. At that time, the victim decided to give the police information about who shot him, because he believed the defendant, apparently unhappy that the victim was still alive after he shot him, was placing flyers in the neighborhood identifying the victim as a sex offender who was living in the neighborhood. The defendant was arrested, and the victim picked him out of a lineup despite previously telling the police that he did not see the shooter's face.

When being placed in the lineup the defendant at first refused to participate, saying he was not involved in any robberies. When told the lineup concerned a shooting, not a robbery, the defendant said, "The one on Parkside? I saw that guy. He's 'street.' He won't pick me." Well, the victim picked him, and the defendant was convicted of attempted murder and unlawful possession of a gun.

Sometimes, despite how much a jury may not like a victim's unsavory past behavior, they will, nevertheless, convict if they find the defendant's own actions overcome their negative feelings about the victim.

HE DID IT ON VIDEO AND ADMITTED TO IT ON THE PHONE

People v. Fred Harris (5515/09)

The victim was sitting in his car parked in front of a housing project with his son, his friend, and his friend's son. They had stopped to see another friend who lived there. On telephoning from the parked car, they learned their friend was not home. While parked, a small crowd gathered around their car including one man with an Afro, a white tee shirt, and black pants who was staring into the car. Why this crowd gathered was never explained during the trial.

The man walked away, and a few minutes later the car drove off. As the car was driving away, gunshots were heard. The victim, sitting in the front passenger seat, was shot in his face and neck by bullets traveling through the driver's side window. Multiple surgeries were required to reconstruct his face.

Video surveillance cameras in the housing project were examined by the police. They showed a person at various points around the building who resembled the defendant and fit the witnesses' descriptions of the man who had been staring at their car. One of these cameras actually showed this person standing near the parked car.

Time stamps on the various video cameras showed this person leaving the vicinity of the car, going to another part of the building, coming out of a door holding a pistol, walking through the basement to a door which opened to a ramp facing the street, and then holding a cloth over his right hand and extending his right arm in the direction of the street where the victim was shot. The purported shooter was then seen walking back to the lobby where a camera showed a very clear picture of the person's face. This was how the defendant was identified.

These facts illustrate a classic example of a circumstantial evidence case. Even though no witness testified to seeing the defendant actually fire a gun at the victim, the inference to be drawn from these facts is that the defendant was the shooter. However, this evidence leaves open the possibility that the defendant was not the only shooter and that the victim was actually shot by someone else who was not shown on any of the surveillance cameras.

The scenario in this case is sort of a Brooklyn version of the Kennedy assassination, with a "conspiracy theory" argument to be made that the defendant's shots missed, and the victim was actually shot by someone firing from the Brooklyn equivalent of Dallas' "grassy knoll."

There was one more important piece of evidence in the case. The defendant was confined prior to trial in Rikers Island prison where he was permitted to make outgoing telephone calls.

The prisoners are informed by prominent signs and in a booklet given to all prisoners that these calls are recorded.

Recordings of prisoner calls are routinely made as a security measure, not to gather evidence against the person making the call. Since the advent of digital recording, it has become much easier to store these calls and retrieve them by using the identification number given to each prisoner that must be used before making the outgoing call.

In preparing this case for trial, the prosecution reviewed the defendant's Rikers telephone calls. Played for the jury was a call made with the defendant's identification number telling a family member that the video "only" showed him with a gun but not shooting it.

The defendant testified which allowed the jury to learn he had prior felony convictions for selling crack and possession of a gun. The jury was instructed that these convictions were to be used solely to evaluate the defendant's credibility as a witness and not for purposes of considering whether he had a propensity to commit crimes. The defendant admitted that his voice was on the other recorded telephone calls made to his family using his identification number, but he maintained in his testimony that he was not the person speaking on the telephone call who said he was "only" holding a gun but not shooting it.

The defendant testified that the person making the statement about the gun was another prisoner unknown to him who must have "borrowed" his identification number when making that telephone call. The jury was able to hear the recorded voices in the several telephone calls made to the defendant's family all of which, except one, the defendant conceded was his voice. The jury also heard the defendant's voice when he testified.

The defendant also testified that although he was the person shown in the videos, he was only pointing a cloth at the victim as depicted in the video and was not holding a gun under it.

It seemed every explanation the defendant gave in his testimony only made things worse for him. The defendant was convicted of attempted murder, assault, and other related charges.

THE VICTIM HAD FOUR LEGS AND FUR

People v. Mujahid Alvarez (1146/10)

With all the killing and mayhem that goes on in Brooklyn, this trial involved an assault on a cat named "Juice." Although Juice was seriously injured, he fully recovered.

Animal cruelty cases often receive more attention in the media and attract more demonstrators outside the courthouse seeking justice for the animal victim than cases of murder and assault on humans. While animal cruelty cases may deserve special attention, in my opinion, they stand in sad contrast to the far more numerous cases involving death and injury to humans that fly under the public's radar.

Juice lived with two other cats, Chubs and Panther, in a private home in Brooklyn along with their owner, a college student, her live-in boyfriend, and the girl's parents. The parents noticed that Juice was lethargic and took him to a veterinarian. After a series of appointments with specialists, Juice was found to have 11 fractured ribs and 3 fractured teeth which required surgery to repair.

Abuse was suspected by the examining doctors, and the ASPCA was notified. An investigator came to the home and removed Juice to a shelter to protect it against further abuse. The investigator noticed that the two other cats in the home had singed whiskers, possibly from being burned. The investigator made an appointment to speak with the boyfriend.

During the subsequent interview, the investigator asked the boyfriend if he had thrown Juice against a wall. He admitted he did this, but he said this was a "reflex action" after the cat had scratched him. He denied knowing what had happened to the whiskers of the other two cats. Based on his statement about Juice, the boyfriend was arrested and indicted on felony charges of animal cruelty.

The girlfriend, who was Juice's owner, refused to testify for the prosecution. She asserted her Fifth Amendment privilege against self-incrimination. The prosecution could have obtained her testimony by granting her immunity from prosecution for whatever crimes she may have committed in this matter, but chose not to do so. The evidence at the trial about the injuries to Juice came from the girlfriend's parents and the treating veterinarians.

The defendant testified and said that he had falsely told the ASPCA investigators that he had injured Juice. The defendant said that Juice was injured at a party that his girlfriend had at the house during her college intercession period on a day when her parents were not home. She did not have permission to have this party, and he and his girlfriend were afraid that if her parents found out about the party, she would be thrown out of the house along with him.

Further, he testified that he was not at the party, but, rather, at the Kings County Community College library. There were about 15 people expected at the party. When he got home, his girlfriend was drunk and high on drugs. He saw that Juice appeared to be injured. He testified he admitted to the ASPCA causing the injury to

Juice so that his girlfriend could get Juice back from the ASPCA shelter. He testified he did not know his false admission to injuring Juice would result in his being arrested and prosecuted.

The jury found the defendant not guilty.

I believe the jury really wanted to hear from the girlfriend who, according to the testimony, was the one who knew the truth about what happened and was the central figure in the case. The reason why the girlfriend did not testify was not made known to the jury, because the prosecution did not call her as a witness.

The prosecution was literally in a "no-win" situation. Because she had refused to testify based on a claim that doing so would require her to implicate herself in a crime, the only way to obtain her testimony would be to give her immunity for whatever criminal acts she may committed in this matter. But if this were done, the girlfriend would be able to take exclusive responsibility for injuring Juice and exonerate her boyfriend. Even though the prosecution may have believed that such testimony would be false, it had no witnesses available who could prove its falsity so as to be able to convict her of perjury for falsely exonerating her boyfriend.

Being that the jury was aware that the cat fully recovered and belonged to the girlfriend, and the defendant's testimony was plausible, it seems the jury was not willing to convict the defendant in the absence of the girlfriend's testimony to refute the defendant's testimony.

TWO VERSIONS OF WHO DID WHAT TO WHOM

People v. Michael Tucker (9685/07)

The question for the jury in this assault case was whether the defendant unjustifiably used a weapon to inflict injury on the unarmed victim, or whether the defendant used only a single punch, which would have been justified if the victim was about to throw the first punch at the defendant.

The defendant and the victim got into an argument on the street. The defendant either punched or struck the victim with a weapon. After being hit with either a fist or a weapon, the victim fell to the ground striking his head on the sidewalk. The victim was taken to the hospital where he died two weeks later.

The defendant was not charged with causing the victim's death. Because there was no evidence that the defendant intended to cause the victim's death and no proof that the injury from the fall caused the victim's death, the defendant was not charged with either murder or manslaughter. Nevertheless, the defendant was charged with Assault in the First Degree based on a serious head injury, which carried a maximum sentence of 25 years. This charge required proof that the defendant used a weapon to injure the victim.

Although the prosecution's witnesses saw the defendant and the victim in an argument, none of them testified to actually seeing the defendant hit the victim with a weapon. One witness testified that the victim was loading his van when the defendant and two other men drove up, got out of the vehicle, and started arguing with the victim.

The defendant had made a statement to the police which was presented to the jury. The defendant said he had been making a delivery in his truck and stopped to intercede in an argument between the victim and two other men, all of whom he knew from the neighborhood. From the corner of his eye, the defendant told the police he saw the victim raise his hand as if to strike him, so he punched the victim once in self-defense.

Under, the law, the facts in the defendant's own statement would not have allowed him to use a weapon (what the law calls "deadly force") to defend himself against the ordinary punch he said the victim was about to use, unless the defendant honestly and reasonably believed his own life was in danger from the victim's threatened act of punching him.

The victim had a skull fracture in two separate places, one on each side of his head. The prosecution's medical expert witnesses, as well as the defendant's medical expert witness, all agreed that two separate impacts were required for these injuries and that neither fracture could have been caused by a blow from a fist.

The New York City Assistant Medical Examiner who performed the autopsy believed that either fracture could have been caused by being struck with a hard object and the other injury could have been caused by the head striking the sidewalk. This was the prosecution's theory on which it based its argument that the defendant had unjustifiably used a weapon to allegedly defend himself.

The defendant called a retired Chief Medical Examiner from Suffolk County as an expert witness. This witness testified that neither fracture was consistent with the victim's head being struck with an object. Rather, the witness testified that the injuries were both consistent with a moving head coming into contact with a stationary object, such as street pavement.

During the trial, the defense made it a point for the jury to learn that the victim's hospital records showed he had a blood-alcohol reading of .09, which is slightly higher than the .08 level establishing that a driver is intoxicated. The paramedic who accompanied the victim to the hospital in an ambulance testified that he smelled the odor of alcohol on the victim's breath. On cross-examination, the defense elicited the paramedic's opinion that as part of his emergency treatment, he assumed the victim had been injured "in a fall from alcohol," thus, possibly placing in the jury's mind the notion that the victim may have hit his head on the sidewalk prior to the defendant's punch which put him down for a second time.

The hospital records also showed that the victim was conscious in the hospital and was noted as being "combative," meaning "not cooperative," and, after neurosurgery, the victim had to be placed in "restraints" and was given medication to prevent alcohol withdrawal symptoms.

Although these facts did nothing to clarify whether the injuries were caused by a weapon, it is facts like these that the defense hopes will cause the jury to be less sympathetic to the victim and his family and, thus, more prone to find a reasonable doubt of the defendant's guilt.

Because the evidence was not clear that the defendant had used a weapon to cause any injury to the victim, the evidence was not sufficient to prove beyond a reasonable doubt that that defendant's single punch of the victim was not justified based on his reasonable belief that the victim was about to hit him first. The defendant was acquitted of all charges.

Chapter 14. *TRIALS WHERE THE POLICE WITNESS THE CRIME*

There is testimony from police officers in virtually every criminal trial even when the police do not witness the crime itself, because there is almost always testimony from the police officer or detective who made the arrest. But in cases where the police actually witness the crime and there is no civilian victim, such as cases involving possession or sale of narcotics, possession of an illegal weapon, or assaults on police officers, there is a different flavor to these cases.

In these cases, the credibility of police officers rather than civilian victims and witnesses is often the central issue. Where the charge involves possession of drugs or guns, there generally is no civilian victim for the jury to sympathize with. Further, in cases involving street level sales of drugs or simple possession of a gun where the gun is not used in another crime, the defendant may not be perceived by jurors as being a physical danger to anyone. The absence of a perception that the defendant is a dangerous person is often an intangible factor when jurors are deliberating.

Although the same definition of "beyond a reasonable doubt" is given to jurors in every criminal case, jurors are more likely to find a defendant guilty where the crime provokes sympathy for the victim or fear in jurors that the defendant is dangerous than when the crime is "victimless" and involves only police officers.

Many jurors have strong positive or negative feelings about the police, and one of the objectives of the attorneys for both sides during the jury selection process, is to ascertain if a potential juror has feelings about the police that would prevent that juror from evaluating the testimony of a police officer with the same even handed judgment as the testimony of a civilian witness.

When I started in the criminal justice system in the early 1970's, it was my perception that the general attitude of most prospective jurors was that police officers are more reliable witnesses than the average civilian. Over the years, I have seen that general opinion shift to the point where if a prospective juror now offers that opinion, which is rarely heard, there is usually an audible collective moan from other prospective jurors seated in the spectator section.

It is because so many prospective jurors are distrustful or have negative attitudes towards the police, that when a police officer is charged with a crime, the officer chooses to waive a jury trial and have a judge decide the case. Where only police officers are witnesses in a case, it is that same pool of jurors who sit in judgment of their credibility as witnesses. Therefore, even when police testimony is not contradicted by other witnesses, juries frequently find a reasonable doubt of guilt in these cases.

Unlike a group of civilian witnesses who may happen to witness a crime, where a group of police officers witness a crime, jurors may suspect that the officers got together before the trial "to get their stories straight." Furthermore, jurors may suspect that police officers are biased against someone who has been arrested and are interested in seeing the defendant convicted to a far greater degree than a "neutral" civilian witness. These juror attitudes may have played a part in the outcomes of the following cases.

GUNSHOTS, A BULLET PROOF VEST, BUT NO GUN

People v. Desmond Julien (8302/12)

The defendant was seen on the street by three plain clothes police officers who were patrolling in an unmarked car. Their assignment, as part of an "Anti-Crime" unit, was to be on the alert for violent street crime and suspicious behavior that would justify stopping and questioning people on the street. There had been a radio dispatch of a report of gunshots fired at 2:30 am in front of a particular address. The police responded to the location by driving the wrong way down a one-way street and saw the defendant standing with two other men looking down the street in the direction traffic normally would come from.

The Sergeant in charge of the group testified he saw the defendant holding a black revolver with what appeared to be a silencer extending from the barrel. The Sergeant testified he told the other two officers, "gun." The unmarked car stopped. The Sergeant testified he identified himself as a police officer and ordered the defendant to drop the gun.

The Sergeant testified the defendant placed his hands in his pants, so when one of the other police officer's exited the car, that officer testified he did not see the defendant's hands or any gun he may have been holding. The defendant then ran into a brownstone building,

The police did not follow the defendant into the building. About two minutes later, the defendant emerged with his empty hands held over his head. The police attempted to handcuff the defendant to place him under arrest, but, according to the police, the defendant struggled and refused to cooperate in this procedure.

Other police arrived at this point and observed the struggle. One of the other officers managed to place handcuffs on the defendant. The defendant was wearing a "body vest," commonly known as a "bullet proof vest," but he did not possess a gun or other weapon.

The police entered one of the building's apartments where the defendant lived. They saw an open window. The rear of the building was searched and a black revolver was found by a police officer under the open window of the defendant's apartment.

The police officer who first saw the gun under the window did not testify at the trial. He was being investigated for committing perjury while testifying in another case, and the prosecution wanted to avoid this issue being raised with the jury in this case. The jury was not told why the officer who found the gun did not testify. I gave the jury a "missing witness" instruction in which I told them they could infer, if they wished, that the reason the officer did not testify was that his testimony would not be helpful to the prosecution.

This instruction is given when there is a witness not called to testify by the prosecution even though that witness is available, "under the control" of the prosecution, meaning that the witness could be expected to cooperate with the prosecution, and has information that is material to the trial and is not cumulative to testimony already produced. The police officer who allegedly found the revolver fit this definition. It was the prosecution's choice not to call that officer as a witness and have the jury given this instruction.

The revolver had five live rounds and one spent shell. No fingerprints were recovered from the gun and there was insufficient DNA on the gun for testing. (This DNA is usually from skin cells transferred to an object by people who touched it.)

Even if the jury believed the Sergeant saw he defendant holding what appeared to be a gun, the prosecution had to prove the loaded and operable gun found under the defendant's window was the same gun the defendant was holding. If the gun found was not the one previously possessed by the defendant, then there was no evidence to show that the gun allegedly possessed by the defendant was actually a real gun that was loaded and operable.

The defendant's grandmother testified that she heard gunshots earlier that evening but never saw the defendant with a gun.

The defendant was acquitted of possessing the gun. The defendant was also acquitted of unlawfully wearing a body vest, because it is not illegal to do so unless it is worn during the commission of another crime involving violence or unlawful possession of a gun. The defendant was, however, convicted of the misdemeanor of Resisting Arrest. What may have helped the jury convict on this charge is that other police officers who were not part of the original group of three police officers, also saw the defendant resisting being handcuffed when they arrived on the scene.

DEFENDANT SHOT IN BACK WHILE SHOOTING AT POLICE

People v.Elijah Foster-Bey (9239/10)

This case involved a shooting of a police officer. The defendant was also shot several times, including once in the buttocks indicating his back was turned to whomever shot him. The case was tried twice, because the first trial resulted in a hung jury.

The defendant was riding a bicycle the wrong way down a one-way street towards three plainclothes Anti-Crime police officers who were patrolling in an unmarked car. According to New York City codes, bicycle riders must obey traffic regulations, so the defendant was subject to receiving a traffic ticket. As the unmarked car approached, the defendant drove his bicycle onto the sidewalk, which is another traffic infraction. One of the police officers called out to the defendant to talk to him. The defendant jumped off the bicycle and ran into a building, a three-story brownstone.

Two officers chased after the defendant, while the third parked the car. At this point, all the defendant had done was illegally ride his bicycle. However, one of the officers testified he saw the defendant holding a gun as he chased the defendant up the stairs of the building. There was testimony that the exit door to the roof had recently been nailed shut to keep trespassers from using the roof to use drugs and hang out.

As the defendant reached the door to the roof and unsuccessfully tried to open it, the police testified the defendant turned and pointed his gun down the stairs at the pursuing officers. Shots were fired and one of the officers was struck in the leg and would have bled to death if another officer had not fashioned a tourniquet out of his belt. The gunshot caused the officer to have a permanent limp and be reassigned in the police department to a desk job. In addition to a gunshot wound in his buttock, the defendant was also shot in the thighs. He was hospitalized, but his injuries were not permanent.

Other police officers quickly arrived on the scene, and one of them recovered a handgun from the foot of the staircase leading to the roof door.

The defendant did not testify, but his attorney contended that the defendant never had a gun and that the police officer who was shot was actually struck by one of the bullets fired either by the other police officers or by his own gun.

Much of the trial concerned police laboratory analysis of the ballistics evidence that was recovered. The prosecution contended this evidence showed three separate guns were fired: the guns belonging to the two pursuing officers and the gun found at the foot of the staircase, which the prosecution contended was the gun fired by the defendant that injured the police officer.

There was also a bullet recovered at the hospital from the leg of the wounded officer. Microscopic comparison of the markings on this bullet with markings on a test bullet fired in the police laboratory from the gun recovered from the staircase, according to the police laboratory examiner's opinion, reflected to a reasonable certainty that both bullets were fired from the same gun, meaning the wounded police officer was not shot by another police officer or by his own gun.

No fingerprints that could be analyzed for comparison were found on the staircase gun. However, the gun was examined by the DNA lab at the Office of the New York City Medical Examiner, which is the lab used by the City in all cases, both civil and criminal, where DNA testing is done. This examination showed that there was a mixture of DNA from the skin cells of two people which, when compared to a DNA sample taken from the defendant after his arrest, showed a very high statistical probability that the defendant's DNA was included in that mixture.

The defense challenged much of this evidence, including the contention that the staircase gun was used to shoot the police officer. This argument was based on the lack of precise hospital records concerning who had custody of the bullet recovered from the leg of the wounded officer. The defense argued that the police, in an effort to frame the defendant for the shooting, switched the bullet recovered at the hospital with a bullet that was test fired from the staircase gun, so that the ballistic markings on both bullets would be the same.

The defense also contended that the skin cells found on the staircase gun that may have matched the defendant's DNA could have been transferred to that gun by a police officer who had first touched the defendant and then touched the gun, thereby picking up the defendant's skin cells and transferring those skin cells to the gun.

The defense also contended that the defendant's buttock wound occurred as the defendant was trying to open the door to the roof and not as he was facing down the stairs as contended by the police. The prosecution answered by arguing that the defendant was turning his body after first firing down the stairs.

Ultimately, the jury at the second trial reached a verdict. It acquitted the defendant of attempting to murder a police officer but did convict the defendant of the serious charges of First Degree Assault and Possession of a Weapon, meaning that although there was a reasonable doubt that the defendant intended to kill a police officer, the jury found he intentionally caused serious physical injury by his unjustified shooting and that he unlawfully possessed a loaded gun.

The defendant was 18 years-old at the time of the shooting. The maximum sentence he could have received, which was requested by the District Attorney's Office, was 40 years by combining the maximum sentences of 25 years for the assault charge and15 years for the gun possession charge. I sentenced him to 25 years on the assault charge and 5 years on the gun charge, to run consecutively, for a total of 30 years.

POLICE TESTIMONY WAS NOT ENOUGH

People v. Patrick Miller (8660/07)

Two police officers and their Sergeant were in plain clothes in an unmarked car working in an Anti-Crime unit. At about 11:15 pm, the Sergeant was seated in the front passenger seat. He testified that he saw the defendant on the sidewalk with an "L-shaped bulge" in his waistband, which the Sergeant believed was the outline of a gun. The Sergeant called out to the defendant and asked "for a moment of his time." The defendant, in response, pulled out a handgun, which, at that point, was also observed by the police officer who was driving the car.

The defendant ran and was pursued by the Sergeant and a third officer who had been seated in the rear of the vehicle. The defendant ran into a building and into a first-floor apartment. The Sergeant pursued close behind and got into a struggle with the defendant in the kitchen of the apartment. According to the Sergeant, they both fell through a stairway door and down the stairs into the basement, and the gun that the defendant had been holding fell out of his hands and slid under a table.

The second officer had followed the Sergeant into the apartment. He entered just as the Sergeant and the defendant fell down the stairs to the basement. He followed them to the basement and assisted the Sergeant in handcuffing the defendant.

The third officer, who had been driving, parked the car and then also went into the apartment. By this time, the defendant was in handcuffs and had been brought back up the stairs. The Sergeant told the third officer that there was a gun on the floor of the basement. This officer then went down into the basement and found a loaded semi-automatic pistol on the basement floor.

The police did not request that the gun be examined for fingerprints or DNA. At the time of this 2007 arrest, these tests were not as routinely done as they were later to become, particularly in cases where the person arrested was seen in actual possession of the gun. Nevertheless, the jury was made aware that these tests were not requested by the arresting officers.

The police testified that although they had chased someone into a building, they did not make a radio call to let other officers know where they were going and to ask for "back-up" assistance, because "there was no time to do this."

The Sergeant denied kicking in the apartment door, denied finding the defendant hiding in the basement, and denied actually finding the gun in a kitchen cabinet. No one testified that these events actually happened, but sometimes just asking these questions plants seeds of doubt in the minds of some jurors. This is especially so where jurors may have a general distrust of police testimony.

The defendant did not testify, so the police testimony was not contradicted by any witness. Had the defendant testified, the prosecution, based on my pre-trial ruling, would have been permitted to ask the defendant about his prior conviction for petit larceny arising out of a robbery of a delivery man. I had ruled that the prosecution would not be permitted to ask the defendant about domestic violence incidents against his parents supposedly to obtain money from them to buy marijuana.

145

The most serious charge was possession of a loaded gun on the street, which carried a maximum sentence of 15 years. The jury found the defendant not guilty of this charge, but did convict him of possessing a gun in his home, which was a misdemeanor carrying a maximum one-year sentence. This verdict could have been based on a reasonable doubt that the gun recovered in the house was the same gun the defendant possessed on the street, or simply based on a compromise between those jurors who either did, or did not, believe the police officers.

"THE OFFICER WHO POSTED TOO MUCH ON MYSPACE"

People v. Gary Waters (1050/07)

This seemingly straightforward case in which the defendant was arrested in possession of a loaded gun after being stopped by plainclothes officers resulted in a March 10, 2009 New York Times story by Jim Dwyer about this trial with the headline: "The Officer Who Posted Too Much on MySpace."

At the trial, two plainclothes officers working undercover as a Yellow Cab driver and passenger testified that the defendant sped by their cab on a motorcycle while weaving in and out of traffic. The police followed in their cab, and when the defendant stopped for a red light, the cab cut in front of him so he could not move.

The defendant dropped the motorcycle and fled on foot. The police pursued and caught him climbing a fence. The defendant struggled with the officers, who, after spraying the defendant with Mace, were able to place him in handcuffs. During the struggle, a fanny pack allegedly fell from the defendant and was brought back to the precinct. The fanny pack was opened in front of the desk Sergeant and was found to contain a loaded handgun and multiple additional rounds of ammunition. The defendant had been driving with a suspended driver's license and had four prior felony convictions involving robbery, burglary, and drug possession.

Although the defendant did not testify or present any evidence, his attorney argued that the police planted the gun on the defendant to cover up their excessive use of force in making the arrest which had resulted in the defendant sustaining three broken ribs. No scientific testing was done on the gun to see if it contained the defendant's fingerprints or DNA, this being 2006 when such testing was not done when a gun was found in the possession of the person arrested.

One of the officers involved in this arrest had previously been suspended for 30 days and placed on restricted duty for a year after the police department became aware that he had illegally obtained steroids from a pharmacy to enhance his body building. This pharmacy had been the subject of an investigation for illegally dispensing steroids, and its records showed that this officer had illegally obtained steroids from there.

The jury was made aware of this as well as certain Internet postings by this officer. The defense attorney's research disclosed that on the day before this trial was scheduled to start, the officer noted on his MySpace page that his mood was "Devious." This certainly got the attention of the jurors.

Further, on the officer's Facebook page, he noted his "status" as watching the movie "Training Day" to "brush up on proper police procedure." That movie, which was well-known at the time of this trial, starred Denzel Washington as a brutal and corrupt

Los Angeles police officer, probably the worst possible example for a police officer to emulate.

In addition, this officer posted a comment on a YouTube video which showed a police officer beating up a handcuffed civilian. The officer's comment was that the officer in the video should have beaten up the civilian before handcuffing him to avoid getting into trouble and, as long as he was going to get into trouble, he should have hit the civilian harder.

The jury found the defendant not guilty of possessing the gun but convicted him of the misdemeanor or Resisting Arrest.

The officer who was the subject of the article was interviewed by the reporter after the verdict. Referring to his Internet posts, the officer said, "It paints a picture of a person who could be overly aggressive. You put that together, it's reasonable doubt in anybody's mind." I wonder how many people who read this article later served as jurors in criminal cases and what effect, if any, it had on their view of the police testimony in those cases.

WHEN YOU GOTTA GO, YOU STILL GOTTA WAIT
People v. Laverne Dobbison (6761/06)

In this case, a female driver for Access-A-Ride, a publicly franchised transportation service for the disabled, was charged with assault and Resisting Arrest. The incident began as a team of three plainclothes police officers in an Anti-Crime unit were returning to their precinct at the end of their shift. A parked car was blocking the driveway to the precinct. In the car were two children who told the police their mother had gone across the street to the liquor store.

Parking one's car blocking the driveway of a police precinct and leaving two children in the car to go to liquor store certainly does not show good judgment, but the mother who did this is not the defendant in this case.

Because there were no parking spots available for the police, they double-parked their car in the single traffic lane of the two-way street in order to speak with the children and ascertain why they were left alone in their car. As the police were waiting for the mother to return, the driver of an Access-A-Ride van which was in the line of cars that had formed behind the double-parked police car began honking its horn. The defendant was the driver of the van. She shouted out of the window, that the police should move their "fucking car" because she "had to pee."

One of the officers approached the defendant's van and told her she had to wait, because they were investigating a car containing children and no adult. At that time, the children's mother came running out of the liquor store, apologized, and drove away.

Before the police had a chance to move their car into the driveway, the defendant pulled her van out of the line of cars and drove into the opposite traffic lane. In doing this, the side mirror of defendant's van grazed one of the officers in the shoulder. The three officers then pursued the van in their car and pulled it over a few blocks away.

The defendant refused to comply with the police order to get out of her van. A supervisor was called to the scene to speak with the defendant, and she maintained her refusal to get out of the van.

One of the officers reached into the driver's side window to unlock and open the door, at which time the defendant bit the officer's arm.

This bite constituted the basis of a felony assault charge against the defendant for causing physical injury to a police officer with the intention of preventing that officer from performing a lawful duty as well as a misdemeanor assault charge for intentionally injuring the officer. The officer then punched the defendant on the side of her face. She was removed from the van and handcuffed after a brief struggle which constituted the basis for a Resisting Arrest charge.

The extent of the injury caused by the bite was an issue in the case. The crime of assault requires that "physical injury" be caused, which is defined as "impairment of a bodily function" or "substantial pain." The officer testified that the bite hurt for two days, that it was "black and blue" for about five days, and that he could not work for two days because of the bite to his arm. However, there was no testimony that he took any medication for the alleged pain.

One of the Emergency Medical Technicians who was called to the precinct to treat the bite testified that he heard the defendant yelling profanities from her cell and say that she had AIDS and hoped the officer died from her bite. The defense requested that I exclude as unduly prejudicial the defendant's remark about having AIDS, which was not true.

I allowed the jury to hear what the defendant said as well as informing the jury that the defendant did not have AIDS, because those words tended to show she had an animosity towards the officer which the jury could consider on the question of whether she intended to injure the officer when she bit him.

150

I also allowed the defense to bring out evidence that while in the jail cell, the defendant apparently urinated and wet herself as evidence as to why she was so impatient with the police car blocking her van.

The jury found the defendant not guilty of the felony assault, apparently finding that the bite did not actually cause physical injury. However, the jury found the defendant guilty of attempted assault as a misdemeanor, in that she tried to injure the officer by biting him, as well as finding her guilty of Resisting Arrest. She could have received up to one year in jail. I sentenced her to 30 days in jail and three years of probation.

Chapter 15. *FRAUD TRIALS*

THREE UNLICENSED NURSING SCHOOLS AND 2 TRIALS

People v. Robinson Akenami, Jocelyn Allrich, Nadage August, Salvatrice Gaston, Rodye Paquiot, and Jude Vales (2555/11)

These trials involved six defendants who were charged with a conspiracy to defraud students by operating three unlicensed nursing schools which claimed that graduation from their schools, even though they were not licensed, would qualify their graduates to become licensed practical nurses. Because of the number of defendants, the large number of defrauded students who testified about the individual schools they attended, and the complexity of the individual cases, the six defendants were divided into two groups of three, and a separate trial was held for each group of three.

The case was investigated and prosecuted by the Office of the New York State Attorney General which has the authority, along with the District Attorney of each county in the State, to prosecute crimes of all types. Generally, the Attorney General's Office becomes involved in large scale consumer fraud cases such as this one.

The first trial involved two of the three schools, each operated by one of the defendants. The third defendant in that trial was an employee of one of the schools.

The second trial involved the third school operated by a fourth defendant. A fifth defendant was an employee of that school. The sixth defendant was the alleged mastermind of the entire scheme and was related by marriage to the operator of the school involved in the second trial.

The scheme allegedly involved an arrangement with the principal of a nursing school in Jamaica, West Indies, to provide fraudulent diplomas and transcripts from his school to the students in New York. These documents would purportedly qualify the students in all three schools to sit for the New York licensing exam for practical nurses. These Jamaica documents would reflect that the New York students were graduates of the Jamaica school. The principal of the Jamaica school died while this case was being investigated and was never charged for his part in this scheme.

On their enrollment, it was explained to the students that the New York "schools" were merely test preparation programs and that the students would be receiving their diplomas from a nursing school in Jamaica which was "affiliated" with the New York program in which they were enrolled and to which they paid thousands of dollars in tuition to attend.

However, as the evidence showed, the students were never enrolled in the Jamaica school and did not actually take the courses reflected in their transcripts from the Jamaica school.

The evidence also showed that the schools in New York did not provide the specific courses, the number of course hours, or the required number of hours of supervised training in an actual medical facility that New York required as prerequisites to take the nursing license examination even though the fraudulent "transcripts" from the Jamaica school, if true, would have been sufficient to qualify the students to take the exam.

The defendants essentially claimed that these students were involved in "distance learning" from the Jamaica school and should have been eligible to take the New York nursing licensing examination, and, if there was a problem with their eligibility to take the examination, they were unaware of this problem, and, therefore, had no intent to defraud their students.

The "mastermind" at his trial, claimed that he had a legitimate relationship with the school in Jamaica and that it was the fault of the operators of the three schools that their respective educational programs were deficient resulting in the New York authorities not allowing the students to take the licensing examination.

The school owners were able to obtain dozens of students to enroll in their schools, because the tuition, although amounting to tens of thousands of dollars, was lower than what licensed nursing schools in New York were charging. Furthermore, the students were allowed to pay their tuition on a week by week basis. If they fell behind in their payments, they were suspended until they brought their accounts up to date. Missed class hours were not a problem as long as the tuition payments were made.

Each of the three New York schools enrolled dozens of students, charging them tuition of upwards of $20,000 for a two-year course that was geared to have them pass the licensing examination. However, as noted, these schools did not offer the required number of class hours in many of the required courses and did not provide the requisite supervised experience in an actual medical facility.

Some schools had their students practice their techniques on mannequins and spend time, although less than the required number of hours, shadowing caregivers in a nursing home in the Bronx or in a hospital in Jamaica which was affiliated with the Jamaica nursing school. Money was passed from the schools to the nursing home and to the Jamaican hospital to allow the students to spend time there, which was necessary for the students to believe they were participating in a legitimate educational program.

One of the schools chartered a flights to Jamaica for its students to spend a one-week rotation observing nurses in the Jamaican hospital. This trip was used as a recruiting tool for that school. On the trip, the organizers never allowed their students to have contact with the students actually enrolled in the Jamaica nursing school in which they also were purportedly enrolled.

Most of the students at these schools were already working in the health field as nurses' aides and attended their classes at nights or on weekends in their efforts to upgrade their qualifications and salary. Many of the students took out high-interest loans to pay the tuition, because the schools they attended did not offer financial aid and did not qualify to participate in student loan programs. The students' individual stories were heartbreaking and, at times, brought some jurors to tears.

The schools obtained their students by advertising in newspapers popular in the Caribbean-American community, which was the ethnic background of all of the defendants as well as many of their students. A defendant who operated one of these schools called herself an "international nurse," in her advertisements for her school as well as on her local cable television program where she also promoted a line of beauty products.

After two years of enrollment in these schools, the first group of students "graduated" with their Jamaican credentials. However, the State Education Department would not issue the papers necessary for them to sit for the licensing examination. The students were not told by the authorities why their applications were "put on hold" to check their credentials. Meanwhile, even though their students were not allowed to take the licensing examination, more students were being enrolled in these schools and continued to be defrauded.

Perhaps to avoid litigation, the State did not immediately take steps to shut down these bogus schools. Instead, the Department of Education "investigated" these schools, a process that included sending an undercover investigator to the schools posing as a student. This investigator secretly recorded the student enrollment process, during which each of the schools used the same sales pitch, stating that the students were enrolling in a tutorial service and that diplomas would be issued from the Jamaican school.

Some students who were not allowed to take the licensing exam were given refunds by the defendants, but most were given a runaround by the schools, which claimed not to know why their students were not being allowed to sit for the examination. The schools tried to make arrangements for the students to take the examination in other states but those efforts were not successful. One defendant even tried to get diplomas and transcripts from a nursing school in Panama for her students so that these students would be allowed to sit for the licensing exam.

It was revealed during the trial of the second group of defendants that the mastermind of this scheme was the one who was responsible for instigating the State's investigation. He had sent an anonymous letter to the State Education Department accusing one of the schools of fraudulently using diplomas and transcripts from the Jamaican school. The reason he exposed his own scheme, without naming himself as part of it, was that the operator of that school had stopped paying the mastermind his fee for providing the Jamaican diplomas, because the operator believed these fraudulent documents could be obtained directly from Jamaica without the assistance of the mastermind.

However, what the State Education Department did in response to this letter was put a "hold" on any applicant for a nursing license who claimed to have graduated from the Jamaican school, thereby stopping the students at all three of the schools from taking the examination in New York.

Dozens of defrauded students testified in the two trials in this case. It was really sad to hear how these hardworking and sincere people lost their money and their time due to this scheme. Perhaps some of them knew that they were not actually receiving the education they needed to qualify to take the examination. However, most of these students were not sophisticated and trusted the school administrators, because, as some testified, they were fellow countrymen.

All three operators and the two employees of the schools were convicted. Their defense was that they believed their students were legitimately enrolled in the Jamaican school, but the evidence showed that they knew their schools were not providing the education required for they student to legitimately qualify to take the nursing license exam.

However, the mastermind was acquitted. He testified, without refutation by the prosecution, that he had established similar "distance learning" schools in other states which were "affiliated" with the Jamaican school and that those students were now licensed in those states. His testimony was that the operators of the schools in this case did not follow his instructions as to how to operate the New York schools, which were called "test preparation" centers, because they were not licensed as "schools."

If corners were cut or if misrepresentations were made to the students, he testified he was not responsible, because he was not an owner of these schools and did not supervise their operation. He also testified that he informed the New York authorities about one of the schools when he learned the school was not providing the education required to qualify its students to take the examination. He denied that he informed the State about this school in response to the owner stopping payments to him.

The five convicted defendants all received prison sentences. The two convicted employees received lesser sentences than their respective employers. None of the convicted defendants were in a financial position to make restitution to any of their victims. The tuition money they collected was spent on expenses to run the schools and on refunds to disgruntled students.

There, in fact, were efforts made at these schools to teach the students the material required to pass the examination, even though, if they passed, they would not actually have had the education required by New York State to obtain a license. The defendants may have acted with the intent that their students receive licenses, but they all knew that they were not providing the education required as a prerequisite to take the examination.

It may not have been a perfectly just outcome for the alleged "mastermind" to have been acquitted if, in fact, he was responsible for setting up this scheme and participated in taking a fee for each fraudulent diploma he obtained from the Jamaican school. Sometimes in these types of cases, the prosecution makes a plea arrangement with a lower ranking participant in the scheme for a lesser sentence in return for that person's testimony against another defendant who the prosecution believes is more blameworthy. There was no such arrangement in this case.

This acquittal, in my mind, made sentencing the other defendants more difficult. However, when I thought about how these defendants had no difficulty taking hard-earned tuition money from their students for providing an education that did not qualify them to take the licensing examination, this factor made their sentencing a little more palatable to me.

A POLICE OFFICER'S WIFE COLLECTS WELFARE

People v. Marcia King (5502/09)

The defendant was legally receiving public assistance benefits from New York City for many years. However, when she married a police officer, she allegedly did not notify the Human Resources Administration (HRA) of her marriage. Her husband's income would have disqualified her from continuing to receive benefits. She continued to receive benefits for six years after the marriage, and, as a result, was charged with welfare fraud and grand larceny for receiving approximately $30,000 in payments to which she was not entitled. The prosecution relied on the paperwork submitted to HRA by the defendant and did not call any HRA employees who, according to the records, periodically interviewed the defendant to determine her continued eligibility. The records showed that before she was married, she listed her marital status as "S." In another form, she wrote "single" to indicate her marital status.

After the date of her marriage, the defendant continued to write "S" on the forms. The defense contended this "S" meant she was "separated," from her husband and not receiving any financial support from him. However, when listing the marital status of her children on the same forms, the defendant also wrote "S," which the prosecution argued demonstrated that when the defendant wrote "S," it meant "single" and not "separated."

In addition, the prosecution introduced evidence that the defendant was listed as a dependent on her husband's health insurance. To further prove that the defendant had a continuing marital relationship, the prosecution introduced documents showing that the defendant's mother and the defendant's husband were listed as co-owners of the house in which she lived. The prosecution contended that the defendant listed her mother rather than herself as a co-owner of the house so that the defendant would not have to list the house as an asset on her welfare applications. Despite the evidence that the defendant was receiving financial support from her husband and deliberately did not tell HRA that she was married, the jury found the defendant not guilty of all charges. HRA's own records of the defendant's re-certification applications were so unclear that they did not disclose whether the defendant had in-person, face-to-face, interviews or whether the applications were submitted by mail.

The prosecution's failure to call any HRA employee who had a face-to-face interview with the defendant to affirmatively state that the defendant never told HRA that she was married, or ever told the HRA that she was "single" rather than "separated," apparently was enough for the jury to decide that there was a reasonable doubt that the defendant did not tell an HRA employee that she was married, even though the defendant never testified. This seemed to be a case where once the matter came to the attention of HRA, they rushed to make an arrest on the assumption that they had all the evidence that was needed, rather than have a face-to-face interview with the defendant by someone who would have been prepared to testify in court as to what the defendant said when asked about her marital status.

Chapter 16. *NON-JURY TRIALS*

Defendants charged with a felony have a constitutional right to a jury trial, which in New York consists of 12 jurors who must be unanimous to reach a verdict of either guilty or not guilty. However, there may be situations where a defendant may wish to waive a jury and have a judge reach the verdict. This decision may be made for various reasons.

Sometimes a defendant may believe that there is a legal concept in the case that a judge would be better able to decide, such as the application of the law of self-defense. Sometimes the facts of the case are so graphic or emotionally tinged that a defendant may believe that a judge would better able to put those aspects aside and focus on what the defense believes are the important issues.

For various reasons, the defendants in the following cases waived a jury, and left the verdict in my hands.

DEATH WAS NOT A REASONABLY FORESEEABLE RESULT

People v. Keston Jones and Ruben Santiago (6128/13)

Both defendants waived a jury in this case of murder and robbery. The deceased was a medical doctor who had lost his license due to severe issues with alcohol. His family owned rental properties in Brooklyn, and it was his routine to collect the rent from the tenants.

One afternoon as he was making his rounds, he came across the two defendants and two women drinking on he street. They asked him to join their party. He walked to a nearby liquor store and bought more liquor for the group. This street scene was captured on video surveillance cameras. Although there was no audio, one of the women testified at the trial and provided the details of what was said. The deceased was asked to accompany the group to the roof of one of the buildings, about five stories high, where the party would continue. Other video surveillance cameras captured the group climbing the stairs and drinking on the roof of the building.

On the roof, the women, while dancing with the deceased, pulled the deceased's shirt over his head and persuaded him to take off his pants. While he was distracted and dancing in his underwear, one of the women removed about $400 from his pants which were lying of the floor of the roof. Because this money was not taken by the use of force nor was it taken from the victim's person, and the amount was less than $1000, the crime committed by the woman was petit larceny. The two defendants on trial were not charged with this theft.

The group of four then left the deceased alone on the roof. According to the testimony of one of the women who testified as a prosecution witness, the stolen money was split among the four in the group after they left the roof.

While the deceased was alone on the roof, the video surveillance camera showed him walking about the roof and, at several points, walking to the edges of the roof and placing his hands on the two-foot high ledge that surrounded the roof while looking down. Clearly, even though he was obviously intoxicated, the deceased knew he was on a roof and was aware of the low height of the surrounding ledge.

After about a half hour, the two defendants returned without the women. By this time, the sun had set and it was dark. Lights on the roof made the scene visible on the video. The deceased hugged one of defendants as if he was glad to see him. Suddenly, one of the defendants, using an aerosol can, sprayed a substance in the face of the deceased causing him to rub his eyes. The surveillance video actually captured the misty spray being discharged from the can. Both defendants then immediately went through the deceased's pockets, and one of them took his iPhone.

The two defendants left the roof through the nearby stairway door which did not close behind them. The stairway lights could be seen shining through the open doorway. The deceased is seen staggering around the roof and rubbing his eyes. At other points, he is also seen crawling on the floor of the roof.

The deceased moved out of camera range for about an hour during which time all that is seen on the silent video is the area of the roof showing the open stairway door. When the deceased reappeared, he is seen staggering with his arms outstretched in front of him walking towards the edge of the roof.

Tragically, without slowing down as he approached the edge, he fell over the roof ledge and died from the fall.

The defendants were charged with murder on the theory that they acted with "depraved indifference to human life" (meaning that they did not care whether the deceased lived or died) and "caused" the death of the deceased by leaving him on the roof in an intoxicated and blinded condition.

The defendants were also charged with a second count of murder, commonly known as "felony murder," under the theory that during the course of a robbery, they "caused" the death of the deceased.

The major legal issue under both counts of murder was whether the defendants were legally responsible for "causing" the death of the deceased. Clearly, if the defendants had not done what they did, the deceased would not have fallen off the roof, but that is not the test for determining legal causation.

The test for legal causation is whether the death was "reasonably foreseeable" and this had to be proven beyond a reasonable doubt. For example, legal causation for "depraved indifference" murder has been found in a case where an intoxicated person was taken to a rural area in a snow storm and left by an unlit road where, twenty minutes later, while helplessly sitting in the road, he was killed by a speeding truck. Also, in a case of felony murder, a robber who fled by jumping across rooftops was held responsible for causing the death of a police officer who pursued him and fell between rooftops during the chase. In both of these examples, the deaths were found be reasonably foreseeable.

However, in this case, before his face was sprayed, the deceased was aware that he was on a roof with a two-foot high ledge and was able to walk around it safely when he was intoxicated. Further, the defendants had left the stairway door open with a light shining through it. Additionally, the Medical Examiner was unable to determine the precise nature of the substance sprayed in the deceased's face, and there was no evidence to establish that the defendants were aware of how long the blinding effect of the spray would last.

Therefore, I found the defendants not guilty of both murder charges based on the lack of proof beyond a reasonable doubt that it was reasonably foreseeable that the defendants' actions would result in the deceased falling off the roof. The surveillance video showed that the deceased was aware that the roof had a two-foot-high ledge before his face was sprayed, and there was no evidence to show that the defendants would have any reason to believe that their actions would cause him to forget the danger he knew to exist by walking on that roof without seeing where he was going.

Even if the deceased could not see where he was going, there was no evidence to indicate that the defendants knew that the deceased would not just crawl around the roof until he found the open door leading to the stairs or just yell for help until someone came to his assistance.

However, I did find both defendants guilty of forcibly stealing the victim's iPhone, which constituted Robbery in the Second Degree based on their being more than one participant in the robbery and imposed the maximum 15-year sentence on that charge.

THE DRIVER CLAIMED HE HAD A SEIZURE

People v. Jermaine Filmore (221/12)

This trial involved a charge of reckless manslaughter resulting from a traffic fatality where the defendant was speeding in excess of 70 miles per hour on the wrong side of Eastern Parkway, a heavily trafficked six lane street. The defendant drove through two red lights and was driving in a zebra striped section of the roadway separating the two directions of traffic.

As he approached the intersection, the zebra striped section changed into a left turn lane. The defendant swerved to avoid hitting a car stopped in the left turn lane and went through a red light at the intersection, striking the deceased's car, which was traveling through a green light on the cross street and sending it crashing into a light pole where it burst into flames. This horrific crash was recorded on a surveillance camera.

After the impact, the defendant's car crashed into a second car which was stopped at the light in the opposite direction injuring the driver of that car. The defendant was unhurt and was arrested at the scene.

The defendant, who was driving home from work as a security guard at the nearby Brooklyn Public Library at the time of this 9:30 pm incident, had a history of epileptic seizures. His defense claimed he was not legally responsible for his apparent reckless driving, because he was having a seizure at the time and had no ability to control, or even remember, his driving at that time.

Each side at the trial called psychiatrists who had examined the defendant after the incident. The defendant also called the psychiatrist who had treated him for an epileptic seizure about two

166

years before this incident during which he was also involved in a non-fatal automobile crash while driving.

There may have been a legal basis to charge the defendant for reckless manslaughter for driving knowing he was subject to having seizures. Under this theory of prosecution, the defendant would be responsible for recklessly causing the death of another person if had an epileptic seizure at the time. However, it was the prosecution's contention that the defendant did not have a seizure at the time of the crash in this case and was simply speeding and driving recklessly in order to get home from work as quickly as he could.

The attorneys for both sides focused on the most minute details of the defendant's driving that night and his behavior immediately after the crash in order to establish their respective contentions concerning whether he was, or was not, conscious of what he was doing when he was speeding and weaving in and out of traffic lanes.

Ultimately, I concluded that the defendant's maneuvers while he was speeding for three blocks down Eastern Parkway, including several lane changes to avoid slower moving vehicles, reflected beyond a reasonable doubt that he was consciously controlling his vehicle and was not having a seizure at the time. Although there was no evidence of skid marks or other evidence that the defendant had applied the brakes before the crash, which the defense contended showed that the defendant was not aware of what was happening, I concluded that the lack of braking was consistent with the defendant not seeing the deceased's car cross his path until just before impact and that his high rate of speed did not allow for time to apply the brakes before hitting the deceased's car.

I found the defendant guilty of reckless manslaughter rather than the lesser charge of criminally negligent homicide, because the evidence established that the defendant was aware of and consciously disregarded the substantial risk of death he was creating rather than merely negligently failing to see that his actions created a substantial risk of death.

TWO TRIALS AND THE DEATH OF A LITTLE GIRL

People v. Jason Marcel and Jillian Rodney (1220/07)

In this sad case, a three year-old girl was killed by her father. The father was living with his girlfriend who was also charged with responsibility for the child's death. Both defendants waived a jury, perhaps because each believed that, in view of the horrific facts of the girl's death, a jury would not give them a fair trial.

Each defendant was entitled to a separate trial, because they both made statements to the authorities implicating the other defendant. In particular, the girlfriend's statements placed the entire blame on the father. Because the prosecution wished to use these statements at trial including the parts where each defendant implicated the other defendant, the defendant implicated in the co-defendant's statement would be entitled to a separate trial based on the fact that the defendant implicated by the co-defendant's statement would not have an opportunity to cross-examine the co-defendant who made the statement.

To better understand this concept, hypothetically assume that two people, A and B, are arrested for committing a crime, and A admits to the police committing the crime with B. If both defendants are on trial in front of the same jury and the prosecution wishes to introduce A's entire statement into evidence through the testimony of the police officer who spoke with A, defendant B, who did not make the statement, would not have the opportunity to cross-examine defendant A as to the truth of defendant A's accusation. Under these circumstances, defendant B, who did not make the statement, would be entitled to a separate trial where the jury would not hear the statement made by defendant A.

In this case, the father, Jason Marcel, went to trial first and waived a jury. He had admitted to the authorities in several statements that he had caused the injuries resulting in the child's death. Prior to the trial, I held a hearing to determine whether these statements would be admissible in evidence at the trial or whether the statements would not be allowed, either because some of them were made without the defendant being advised of his right to remain silent and his other *Miranda* rights, or, when at a later time when he was advised of his rights, the defendant believed it would be useless to refuse to answer questions because he had already incriminated himself, thus making the later statements also inadmissible.

For the reasons I will discuss below, I ruled the statements to be admissible. Therefore, because it would have been difficult for Marcel to dispute at trial that he had caused the child's death, his best defense would be that he did not have the criminal intent required for the most serious charges. Due to the child's horrific injuries, a jury would have had little sympathy for him, and, perhaps therefore, not pay attention to the technical legal distinctions between the greater and lesser charges. Accordingly, Marcel followed his attorney's advice and waived a jury trial where a judge, presumably, would be better able to analyze the legal aspects of the case.

The deceased girl usually lived with her mother, but six months before the child's death, her mother dropped the child off with Marcel, telling him she would pick the child up in a few days. Instead, the mother never came back for the child and only occasionally spoke with the child on the telephone.

The police became involved after Marcel called an ambulance to take his unconscious three year-old daughter to the hospital. The child had severe burns on her feet that were slowly healing. Marcel said the child had accidentally burned her feet when she turned on the hot water while taking a bath. To another police officer, Marcel said the child's mother had dropped her off with the severe burns. He said he believed that if he brought the child to the hospital for the burns, he would get in trouble for child abuse, so he treated the burns himself with ointment.

Marcel said he did not know why the child was unconscious. He told a detective at the hospital that he had fallen asleep while watching television, and when he awoke, the child was unconscious. He tried to revive the child by performing CPR but that did not help. He told this detective that the child had previously burned her feet with hot water from a kettle that was left on the stove.

At the hearing prior to trial, I ruled that all of these statements would be admissible even though *Miranda* rights were not given, because those rights are only required where a person is "in custody," meaning that a reasonable person, innocent of any crime, under the circumstances would not feel free to leave. In this case, Marcel was a person who voluntarily brought his child to the hospital and was simply questioned about what happened to the child. He was not placed under arrest at that time, and was never told prior to making these statements that he could not leave the hospital.

Marcel agreed to go to the police station with one of the detectives. At the police station, he was given his *Miranda* rights by the detective and later by an Assistant District Attorney. Marcel made statements to both of them which I also ruled would be admissible at the trial. At the time of the questioning in the police station, the specific cause of the child's death had not been determined. An autopsy had not yet been done.

According to the Marcel's statements at the police station, the child, beginning about three weeks before, often deliberately urinated on the floor rather than in her potty. When she did this, Marcel said he would "hit her on the butt" with an open hand. He believed the misbehavior was because she "missed her mother." On this night, the child seemed to faint as he was preparing her for a bath, and then she started vomiting. He believed that when the child fainted, she hit her head on the bathtub faucet.

He was preparing the bath, because the child had spread her feces in the bedroom and the bathroom. She had also done this previously about three weeks before. At that time, Marcel said he poured hot water on her feet which was actually how she got the burns. At that time, he asked a friend to go on-line to look up how to treat the burns.

The burns were starting get better, but the child would tamper with the bandages to make the burns bleed. When she did this, he said hit the child on her back, butt, and shoulders.

At the trial, a physician who specialized in child abuse cases was called as an expert witness regarding the burns to the child's feet, photographs of which were admitted in evidence. In the opinion of this witness, the burn marks were consistent with the feet being held under hot water, because the burns were in a straight line on the leg and also present on the bottom of the feet. If hot water were poured on the child, it would produce "arrowhead" shaped burns consistent with water running down the leg.

The Medical Examiner testified that the actual cause of death was a lacerated liver resulting from blunt force causing loss of blood in the abdominal cavity and that there would be only "a few minutes" between the blow and loss of consciousness. The child also had other evidence of injuries about her body which appeared to have been inflicted within 48 hours of the child's death.

The most serious charge was Murder in the Second Degree which has various definitions. Marcel was not charged with intentionally killing the child which would also be Murder in the Second Degree. In this case, he was charged under a definition of Murder in the Second Degree that required the prosecution to prove that the defendant, being 18 years-old or more, acting "with depraved indifference to human life," caused the death of a child less than 11 years-old by "recklessly engaging in conduct which created a grave risk of serious physical injury to the child."

The central issue was whether the defendant acted with "depraved indifference to human life." As interpreted by New York's highest appellate court, that standard does not apply to the circumstances surrounding the defendant's acts, which could readily be found to have been "depraved." Rather, what is required to be shown is that when the defendant struck the child, which was the cause of death, the defendant did not care, one way or the other, whether the child lived or died or intentionally prolonged or intensified the child's suffering from that blow.

Although Marcel may have intentionally caused the child to suffer when he burned her feet with hot water, those acts did not cause or even contribute to the child's death, and there was evidence that the defendant made efforts to ameliorate the child's suffering by treating the burns himself.

I, therefore, found Marcel not guilty of the murder charge. However, I found him guilty of Reckless Manslaughter in the First Degree, because when he struck the child damaging her liver, he acted with intent to cause physical injury to the child and caused the child's death by creating a grave risk of serious physical injury. I also found him guilty of felony assault on the child for intentionally burning her feet with the hot water.

He was sentenced to a total of 18 years in prison for these convictions. The child's biological mother was not charged, although if she had not virtually abandoned her little girl, this never would have happened.

* * * * *

The girlfriend, Jillian Rodney's case went to trial about a year later. She also chose to waive a jury. Because her statements to the police were not in evidence at Marcel's trial, and because his statements were not in evidence at her trial, the "facts" of each case as I heard the evidence were not exactly the same. Her statements to the police implicated Marcel in the child's death, and that is why he was entitled to a separate trial in which her statements would not be in evidence.

The evidence at Rodney's trial showed that she lived with Marcel, her own children, and Marcel's three-year-old daughter. Based on her statements to the police, the evidence showed that

Marcel struck his own daughter lacerating here liver and causing her death.

Rodney, based on her statements to the police, knew that two weeks before the child's death, Marcel had held the child's feet under hot water causing severe burns after the child had smeared her feces on the apartment walls. The prosecution contended Rodney was also responsible for causing the child's death, because she "instigated" Marcel to beat the child by telling him that the child had urinated on the bedroom floor, because she should have known that her Marcel would beat his child if he learned about the child's urinating on the floor. (In Marcel's statement, he said that on the night of the fatal beating the child had spread feces in contrast to Rodney's statement that on that night the child urinated on the floor. Under the rules of evidence, Marcel's statement had to be ignored at Rodney's trial.)

The evidence of this history of abuse was based on Rodney's statements to the police during their investigation into the death of the child. Therefore, at her trial, Rodney could not plausibly dispute having prior knowledge of Marcel's abusive behavior towards the child.

I found Rodney not guilty of all of the charges against her, applying the legal definitions of the crimes charged to the facts in this case. As to the charge of reckless manslaughter, I found that the prosecution had not proven beyond a reasonable doubt that she consciously disregarded a substantial risk of death to the child by merely telling Marcel that his daughter had urinated on the floor, which was the prosecution's basis for this charge.

I found that telling Marcel about his daughter urinating on the floor was not a "gross deviation" from what a reasonable person would have done. In fact, Rodney cleaned the urine from the floor herself before telling Marcel what his daughter had done. Thus, this incident was different from the prior feces incident where Marcel had to clean the mess himself and then, in anger, poured hot water on the child's feet.

Rodney was also found not guilty of criminally negligent homicide, because of a lack of proof that she should have been aware of the substantial risk of death to the child by telling Marcel about his daughter urinating on the floor. Marcel's prior abuse of the child never rose to the level of creating a substantial risk of death to the child, and there was insufficient evidence to establish that Rodney should have known there was a risk of death to the child by telling Marcel what happened after the urine on the floor had been cleaned up.

Rodney was also charged with recklessly endangering the life of the child in the first degree by (1) failing to obtain proper medical attention when the child's feet were burned, (2) failing to intervene Marcel's fatal attack on the child, and (3) thereafter failing to obtain prompt medical attention for the child. These charges required the prosecution to prove that Rodney had a "depraved indifference to human life," meaning, as that definition has been interpreted by New York's highest court, that she virtually did not care whether the child lived or died.

The evidence did not establish that Rodney had this state of mind. She treated the child's burns herself and, in addition, was concerned that if the child died, she would lose custody of her own children. Therefore, she certainly was concerned for the life of the child.

Furthermore, as to the lesser charges of recklessly injuring the child by failing to intervene in the fatal beating and endangering the welfare of a child for failing to obtain medical attention, as harsh as this may seem, there was a reasonable doubt whether she even had a legal duty to perform these acts. Rodney was not the child's parent nor hired as the child's caretaker. The child had been in her apartment on a temporary basis. The child was visiting with Marcel and the poor child's mother refused to take her back. There was no evidence that Rodney ever agreed to assume any parental duties towards the child.

In fact, shortly after the child came into Rodney's home, she gave birth to twins, fathered by Marcel, and one of the twins died two weeks later. From the testimony, it appeared that the Rodney did not want her Marcel's child in her house at all, and, according to her statement, Marcel would not even let her touch the child. Because the evidence showed that Rodney never assumed a parental role towards the child, she had no legal duty to care for the child.

Under New York law, temporarily caring for a child does not establish the required intent to support and care for the child on a permanent basis which is necessary for this legal duty to arise. A conviction in this case could not be based on whatever moral duty the girlfriend may have had towards the child.

There was a different section of the Endangering the Welfare of a Child statute that would have been more applicable to the facts of this case. It is a misdemeanor not to properly care for a child over whom a person has temporary custody, even if that person has not assumed a parental role. Although that statute seemed to apply to the facts of this case, the prosecution did not charge the defendant under that statute.

Even though Rodney was acquitted, Marcel, who was her boyfriend and the father of her surviving twin, had been convicted and sent to prison. In addition, Rodney had lost her own newborn child while these incidents were taking place. She was not really a winner here.

FORGED PAPERS FOR STOLEN CARS

People v. Henry Morel and Nathaniel Urena (3832/11)

This case involved a sophisticated stolen car ring investigated and prosecuted by the New York Attorney General's Office. There were 16 indicted defendants in this case. Fourteen entered guilty pleas, and two waived a jury and went to trial before me.

Designated members of this group would search for late model Toyota vehicles parked on the streets of Brooklyn and look through their windshields to obtain the vehicle identification numbers (VIN) from the plates mounted on their dashboards. The VIN numbers would then be forwarded to a corrupt employee of a Toyota dealership in Brooklyn who would look up the key code that corresponded to that vehicle. The code would then be given to a locksmith who was part of the group, and a key for that vehicle would be made. The vehicle would then be stolen using the key and left parked for a period of time to make sure there was no anti-theft tracking device in the car.

After taking possession of the stolen vehicles, the VIN plates on the dashboard and on other parts of the car would then be altered so as not to correspond to the VIN numbers on the stolen vehicles.

The defendants in this trial had the role of forgers of the registration and titles to these stolen cars using the altered VIN numbers so that the cars could be sold with what appeared to be legitimate ownership papers to unsuspecting buyers. Sometimes, the year the vehicle was manufactured would be changed on the forged papers to make the vehicle "newer" than it actually was so that the thieves could sell it for a higher price.

The investigators in this case obtained court-authorized permission to intercept the phone calls and text messages from the cell phones of the suspects in this case, so at the trial there was evidence of information being passed among the group of defendants concerning the locations of the potential stolen cars, their specific VIN numbers, their license plate numbers, the key codes, and when the forged documentation for these stolen cars would be ready. There was a "pole camera" set up on the street outside the defendants' house to take pictures of some of the other defendants in the case coming to the house to pick up the forged papers at the hours of the day and night corresponding to the times discussed in the intercepted telephone messages.

There really was no question about the defendants' involvement in the scheme. The only real issue at the trial was whether they were guilty of the most serious charge of "Enterprise Corruption" which required that they be shown to have had full knowledge of the entire scheme including the theft of the cars and the illegal duplication of the keys. I found that this aspect was not proven beyond a reasonable doubt. I also found the two defendants not guilty of participating in the thefts of the cars off the streets. Nevertheless, they were found guilty of multiple felony charges of forgery, possession of a forged instrument, and possession of stolen property, because they knew they were assisting in the possession of cars that were stolen, as well as guilty of conspiracy.

Chapter 17. *MURDER TRIALS*

MAYBE THE WITNESS WAS THE ACTUAL KILLER

People v. Tesonn Hendrix and Clifford Thompson (9552/09)

This case involved a shooting in the hallway of a housing project. The prosecution's theory of the case was that the defendant Hendrix, who knew the deceased as a neighborhood drug dealer, planned with co-defendant Thompson and an accomplice, named Tolar, to rob the drug dealer by setting up a phony drug sale. Hendrix would contact the drug dealer to arrange the purported drug sale. Tolar would pretend to be the drug seller, and at the time when the drug dealer would be exchanging his money for the drugs that Tolar would be pretending to have, Thompson, at a pre-arranged signal, would appear in the hallway and rob the drug dealer. The plan did not include killing anyone.

However, when Thompson appeared in the hallway for the robbery, the drug dealer resisted Thompson's efforts to rob him at gunpoint and, in fact, recognized Thompson's face when Thompson's bandanna mask fell off. Thompson then shot the drug dealer while both were wrestling with the gun. The drug dealer was shot once in the thigh and died from loss of blood.

Because this was a killing during the course of a robbery, the crime is known as "felony murder," making all of the participants in the robbery responsible for the crime of murder, even if the killing was not intentional and even if a participant in the planned robbery was not present.

Information about the planning of this robbery came from the testimony of Tolar, an accomplice in the robbery, who made an arrangement with the prosecution to plead guilty to a lesser charge in return for his testimony. Tolar had been arrested in several other cases as well as this case and offered the police information on this case in return for a "package deal" with a sentence of 12 years to life for all his cases including this case.

One of the reasons the deal was made with Tolar was that he was believed to be the least culpable of the three men, because he did not plan the robbery and he was not the shooter. Because Tolar was an accomplice who participated in the crime, under New York law, the other two defendants could not be convicted solely on Tolar's testimony without other evidence "tending to connect" them to the crime. This means the jury had to find other evidence in the case to corroborate Tolar's testimony that the defendants were involved in the robbery resulting in the death of the victim.

Shortly before the trial was to begin, it came to the attention of the prosecutor that Tolar was linked to another robbery by a fingerprint found on a beer bottle at the scene. This information would put another dent in Tolar's credibility with the jury. Of more significance, that robbery involved a shooting, and ballistics evidence at the scene of that crime matched the ballistics evidence at the scene of this crime, meaning the same gun was used in both cases. This fact gave the defendants attorneys the "ammunition" to argue that because the gun used in this case was linked to Tolar in the other robbery, it was, in fact, Tolar and not the defendant Thompson who had the gun in this case and shot the deceased.

However, when the police first arrived at the scene, the drug dealer was still alive. An officer asked, "Who did it?" The dying drug dealer answered, "the light skinned guy." Thompson clearly had lighter skin than Tolar.

I allowed this statement into evidence at the trial under the "excited utterance" rule which allows into evidence statements made under such stressful circumstances that it is unlikely that the person making the statement had the state of mind to intentionally make something up that was not true. This was a critical ruling against Thompson, because, obviously, the drug dealer was now dead and could not be cross-examined at the trial by Thompson as to what he meant when he said, "the light skinned guy."

Thompson was connected to the crime by video surveillance inside the housing project which showed him entering the building with the drug dealer. However, there was no video surveillance in the area of the hallway where the shooting took place. This was the reason why the defendants picked that location in the building for their planned robbery.

Thompson also made several statements to the police after he was arrested. He admitted to being present with the drug dealer and Tolar for a planned drug deal, but he claimed there was no plan to rob the drug dealer. Thompson claimed to the police that the drug dealer and Tolar got into a struggle during the drug deal, and it was Tolar who shot the drug dealer. Thus, the discovery on the eve of trial of Tolar's involvement in another robbery where the same gun was used now made Thompson's claim that Tolar had the gun in this case more likely.

Hendrix who was not present in the hallway at the time of the shooting was connected to the crime by cell phone records showing numerous text messages between him and the drug dealer on the day of the shooting arranging to meet at the housing project for a drug deal set up by Hendrix. Hendrix also made statements to the police admitting to setting up a drug deal but did not admit to having a plan to rob the drug dealer. Hendrix also told the police that after the shooting, Tolar told him that Thompson "fucked up" and shot the deceased. This statement was heard by the jury in Hendrix's trial, but the jury in Thompson's separate trial did not know about it.

Both Hendrix and Thompson made statements to the police implicating not only themselves, but also each other in the crime. This was a circumstance similar to the case of Marcel and Rodney described in Chapter 16. Under the law, a jury is generally not allowed to hear that part of a defendant's statement to the police implicating a co-defendant who is also being tried. This is because the co-defendant who is implicated would have no opportunity to cross-examine the co-defendant who accused him. The United States Supreme Court has ruled that allowing this type of testimony would violate the co-defendant's constitutional right "to confront his accuser," meaning his right to cross-examine the person who said he committed the crime.

To allow the prosecution to introduce such a statement into evidence against the defendant who made that statement, the co-defendant named in that statement would have to be tried separately by a different jury who would not hear that statement. Where there are many witnesses in a case who would have to testify at two trials, a procedure has been developed where two juries, one for each defendant, hear the case at the same time. When it comes time for a defendant's statement to be introduced into evidence which implicates the co-defendant, the jury hearing the co-defendant's case is sent out of the courtroom. Where the co-defendant, as was the situation in this case, has also made a statement implicating the other defendant, the procedure is reversed, and the other defendant's jury is sent out of the courtroom.

In Brooklyn, because of the significant number of cases falling into this situation, two large courtrooms were constructed to hear cases such as this. These courtrooms have two separate jury boxes, each one holding a full jury for its own defendant.

For most of the trial, witnesses who would otherwise have to testify at two trials can testify once before two juries. The juries are separately picked by each defendant and are not present when the other jury is selected. Only one jury at a time is present for the lawyers' opening statements, summations, and the court's final instructions. They deliberate separately, render their verdicts separately, and each jury does not know the result of the other trial when it announces its verdict.

The jury trying Hendrix found him not guilty. Hendrix testified (out of the presence of Thompson's jury) that all he did was set up a drug deal between the drug dealer and Tolar, and a robbery or a shooting was not part of the plan. The defense for Hendrix argued that Tolar and Thompson may have decided on their own to rob the drug dealer, but Hendrix was not present and did not know that would happen. Apparently, the jury did not find Tolar's testimony that it was Hendrix who planned the robbery to be sufficiently credible. Hendrix was found not guilty of all charges.

The jury in Thompson's case was deadlocked after several days of deliberation, and a mistrial was declared. Thompson's defense had argued that Tolar was the shooter and that Thompson was there just for a drug deal and did not have prior knowledge that Tolar would commit a robbery. Therefore, Thompson was not responsible for the killing under the "felony murder" doctrine, because he did not participate in a robbery even though he was present.

After the hung jury, the case was tried again about six months later with another jury, who, of course, was unaware of what happened the first time the case was tried. Thompson was the only defendant at this trial. The jury was instructed not to speculate about what happened to the case of Hendrix after he was arrested.

The law did not allow that jury to learn that Hendrix had been found not guilty even though Tolar again testified that Hendrix had planned the robbery with him and Thompson. The evidence was essentially the same as the first trial. This time, Thompson was convicted of murder.

It may have been the deceased's dying words naming "the light-skinned guy" as the person who did it that persuaded the jury that Thompson, not Tolar, was the shooter.

A GOOD SAMARITAN BECOMES THE VICTIM

People v. Donald Michel (25/09)

This was another felony-murder trial where if the prosecution could prove both that the defendant was the shooter and intended to kill the deceased during the robbery, the defendant would be subject to a sentence of life without the possibility of parole.

The robbery took place in a cell phone store in the Brighton Beach section Brooklyn. The defendant was one of two defendants charged with the crime. Prior to trial, the co-defendant, who was not alleged to be the shooter, pleaded guilty to a robbery charge in return for a lengthy sentence, but less than the life sentence to which he would have been subject if he would have been convicted of felony-murder.

According to the store owner, two men entered the store. The defendant pulled a gun while the co-defendant grabbed cell phones and put them into a shopping bag. The deceased was a livery cab driver working at a car service that was next door to the cell phone store. The store had a glass front door. Apparently, the deceased saw what was happening in the store, and, from the

184

sidewalk outside the store, held the door shut trying to prevent the two robbers from leaving the store. The door was eventually opened, and the defendant as he fled from the scene shot and killed the deceased.

The shopping bag containing the cell phones was left behind in the store. The Crime Scene Unit thoroughly processed the shopping bag and the dozens of items inside the bag looking for evidence of fingerprints and DNA. To find fingerprints, which consist of bodily oils that are not visible to the naked eye, powder is dusted onto the objects in the hope of revealing what are, essentially, oil stains in the shape of the unique ridges and swirls on a person's fingers and palms. If the dusting reveals traces of these oils, cellophane tape similar to Scotch brand tape is placed on the powdered fingerprint. The possibly identifiable print is lifted onto the tape which is then affixed to a cardboard index card.

In this case, numerous "lifts" on the cards were forwarded to the police laboratory to determine if any of the lifts were "of value" so they could be matched to records of fingerprints on file. It was determined that the fingerprints of both defendants were found on the items from the store. The police then located and arrested both defendants. The store owner identified the defendant at a lineup and pointed him out in court during his trial testimony.

There was DNA found on the shopping bag when it was later examined at the Medical Examiner's Laboratory. It contained a mixture of DNA from several people so neither defendant could be conclusively established to have touched the bag.

The defendant made an oral statement to the police and a video statement to an Assistant District Attorney admitting his participation in the robbery, but he claimed the co-defendant was the shooter. He said he gave the gun to the co-defendant just

185

before they fled the store. The video of the defendant's statement was played for the jury by the prosecution, so the defendant did not have to testify to raise his claim that he was not the shooter.

Because the defendant's video statement also incriminated the defendant to the extent that the defendant admitted participating in the robbery, the prosecution's decision to play the video for the jury was a strategically sound decision even though the video also let the jury know that the defendant denied being the shooter.

An interesting aspect of the case was the analysis of the cell phone records of both perpetrators. The records showed not only that they called each other's phone several times earlier that day, but, also, based on the location of the cell phone towers that picked up the phone calls, their cell phones moved closer and closer to the location of the scene of the crime. At the time of the crime, their cell phones were within a few blocks of the cell phone towers close to the store.

The jury found the defendant not guilty of Murder in the First Degree, which was the charge that carried the sentence of life without parole. Either the jury did not agree that the defendant was the shooter, or they did not find the defendant intended to kill the deceased. The jury did find the defendant guilty of felony-murder, which is Murder in the Second degree, and unlawful possession of a gun. On these convictions, the defendant was sentenced to a combined total of 25 years to life in prison to run consecutively to a sentence of seven years for violating his sentence of probation imposed on a prior case, meaning the defendant would have to serve 32 years before being eligible for parole.

All homicides are sad. The deceased, age 24, lost his life trying to stop a robbery of someone he did not know. I believe the deceased was Muslim, because his mother, who identified his body, testified at the trial through a Farsi interpreter, a language predominantly spoken in Iran. I believe the store owner, based on his name and accent, as well as the location of his store in the Brighton Beach section of Brooklyn, was a Jewish immigrant from Russia, many of whom reside in that section of Brooklyn. Those wishing to broadly restrict immigration from certain countries should realize that some immigrants can be heroes.

A REAL HORROR STORY AND TIRELESS POLICE WORK

People v. Anatoly Valenko (12208/07)

The defendant, a native of Ukraine, was charged with killing his two roommates who had a boyfriend-girlfriend relationship. They had been residents of Russia before coming to Brooklyn. A fourth person lived in the apartment. He may also have been involved in the crime, but this person, as well as the defendant, fled to Russia whose government would not cooperate in extraditing either of them.

Twelve years after the killings, Interpol, an international police organization, received information that the defendant was in the Netherlands. The defendant was taken into custody there and returned to the United States to stand trial.

The trial evidence showed that after November 12,1995, friends of the boyfriend and girlfriend were not able to contact them. One of these friends had gone out to dinner with them on November 12,1995 but could not reach them at home the next day. They were never heard from again. When the friend inquired on the telephone of the defendant as to the whereabouts of his two roommates, the defendant told this friend that they had left town to visit relatives in another state, but he did not know exactly where they had gone.

The defendant then asked this friend for money to pay his roommates' share of the rent. When the friend met the defendant in person the next day to loan him money on behalf of her missing friends, she noticed the defendant had scratches across his forehead. He told her he had been taking kickboxing lessons. When the friend later saw that her friends' car was still parked in the neighborhood, she went to the police to report that her friends were missing.

There was testimony from a hardware store owner that on November 13, 1995, he sold a circular saw to two men with Eastern European accents and that the saw was purchased with a credit card in the name of the missing boyfriend.

A woman from New Jersey testified that on November 14, 1995, she received a call from her boyfriend about a suitcase he found in a park in Essex County, New Jersey. She met her boyfriend in the park and saw that the suitcase contained human torsos. Her boyfriend testified he saw a male, dragging the two suitcases from a car and leave them in the park. From an array of six photographs, he selected the photograph of the defendant's roommate as the person who dragged the suitcases. The suitcases contained the torsos of a male and female but no heads, arms, or legs.

Two days later, another woman was walking her dog on Plum Beach in Brooklyn. She saw what looked like a cut leg floating in the water and called the police. When the police responded, they also found a head floating in the water.

A Brooklyn detective assigned to the case had heard about the bodies found in New Jersey and took the head found on the beach to New Jersey to see if it belonged to either of the torsos. The head seemed to match the male torso. Dental x-rays were taken of the head which were found to match the missing boyfriend's dental records.

A contraceptive device was found in the female torso. The device had a serial number which was traced to a doctor who had the missing female as a patient. However, his records could not establish that he had prescribed that particular device to anyone.

The defendant's apartment was examined by the police Crime Scene Unit. There did not appear to be any visible blood. However, traces of blood were found after certain areas were treated with Luminol, a substance used to detect the presence of blood that is not visible. DNA analysis of the bloodstains found in the apartment were determined to match the DNA from the respective male and female torsos from New Jersey and the female left leg from the beach in Brooklyn.

A New Jersey Medical Examiner's autopsy of the torsos showed both had been stabbed five times and the stomachs of both showed partially digested food indicating they had eaten a few hours before their deaths.

After the bodies had been identified, the police looked for the defendant and his roommate, but they had left the country. The credit card of the deceased boyfriend had also been used to purchase luggage on November 16, 1995.

The landlady of the apartment testified she rented the apartment to the defendant and his friends. The defendant had come to her apartment at about 11:00 pm on November 12, 1995 with cuts and scratches on his hands and his face, and his ear was black in the space where he had worn an earring. The defendant said he had been assaulted and robbed on the street and that his wallet and keys to the apartment had been stolen. The defendant told her he had put an additional lock on the door, because the robbers took his apartment keys and knew his address from his wallet. This story would have allowed the defendant and his roommate time to cut up the bodies and clean the apartment without being interrupted by the landlady.

A friend of the deceased female testified that she recognized a birthmark in a photograph of the neck portion of the female torso as a birthmark that was on the neck of her friend. Because the head of the female was never found and identified, an issue for the jury was whether the female torso was actually the person who the prosecution claimed was one of the murder victims in this case.

Two years after the deaths, the investigating detective learned that the defendant was in Kiev, the capital of Ukraine, but local authorities denied the detective permission to speak with the defendant. The detective also learned that the defendant had applied on November 13, 1995 for permission from the Ukrainian consulate to return to travel there.

Although the other roommate who was also likely involved in this double homicide may still be living in freedom in Russia, the defendant's mistake in leaving Ukraine 12 years after these killings led to his apprehension and conviction. By the time of this trial, many of the law enforcement witnesses who testified had retired but, nevertheless, they came to court to testify about what they had done over a decade before to help investigate this case.

This trial was a classic example of a "circumstantial evidence" case where no eyewitness testified to seeing the defendant commit the crime. Indeed, whether or not there was even a murder of the female alleged to have been killed, was also based on circumstantial evidence concerning the identity of the female torso.

The defendant in this case received a sentence of life without possibility of parole, the only time in my judicial career that I have imposed that sentence.

This case brings to mind the often told story about a murder trial where the body was never found. The defense attorney argued during the trial that the alleged murder victim may actually still be alive. During his summation, the attorney told the jury to look at the courtroom door, because in two minutes the allegedly dead victim would be walking through that door. The jury stared in silence at the door for the full two minutes.

No one came through the door, but the attorney then argued to the jury that because they all waited for two minutes for the victim to come into the courtroom, they must, therefore, have a reasonable doubt about the victim actually being dead.

After the jury quickly convicted the defendant, the attorney spoke with the jury in the hallway and asked how they could find beyond a reasonable doubt that the defendant had actually killed the victim. Their answer was, "Your client was the only person in the courtroom who didn't look at the door."

SAVED BY MY COURT CLERK AND GOOGLE EARTH

People v. Javier Vidal and Jose Vidal (9296/07)

The defendants in this case, a father and son, were charged with Manslaughter in the First Degree rather than Murder in the

Second Degree. In this case, the difference between the two charges is that although both charges require that the defendant cause the death of another person, the murder charge requires an intent to cause another's death, whereas the manslaughter charge requires an intent to cause serious physical injury, but, nevertheless, death results.

The underlying facts of this case are all too typical: a dispute between people who know each other breaks out into a fistfight which then escalates. Without meaning to trivialize the tragedy of what happened, what is memorable about this case is what happened afterwards.

The prosecution's side of the story was that the deceased, who was a drug addict and had narcotics in his system at the time of the incident, went to the defendants' home to retrieve a video game player that he believed Javier Vidal, age 19, had taken after using it in the home of a mutual neighbor. A pushing match ensued in the doorway and both men wound up on the street.

Javier's father, Jose Vidal, joined in the fight. They both punched the deceased who fell to the street where he was kicked in the head by both defendants who were each wearing work boots.

The deceased was taken to the hospital where he was treated for a fractured skull and cranial bleeding. The deceased was in a coma and being fed through a tube inserted directly into his abdomen, because he "could not tolerate" the feeding tube that had been inserted in his throat. There were instructions given, as noted in his hospital records, to bind his hands with restraints so he could not remove the tube.

Sixteen days after being admitted to the hospital, the deceased was found unconscious and holding the feeding tube in his unrestrained left hand. The same tube was reinserted. A new tube was not substituted until the next day. However, one day later, the deceased went into septic shock and died. The "cause of death" according to the Medical Examiner was infection due to the deceased not being able to feed himself as the result of a brain injury.

Thus, even before the defense case, there was an issue for the jury to decide concerning whether the gross negligence of the hospital staff in not following their own doctor's orders to put restraints on the deceased so he would not remove the feeding tube, and then putting the removed, unsterile, tube back into him without substituting a sterile tube, relieved the defendants from criminal responsibility for causing the victim's death.

The jury would have to decide if the negligence in the hospital was so unusual that it could not be foreseen (similar to a fire in a hospital causing a patient's death) and thus be a "supervening intervening cause of death." Even if so, the defendants could still be criminally responsible for the assault that took place.

The defendants presented a different version of what happened during the fight through their own testimony and testimony of their family members. The defendants contended that the deceased punched Javier at the door and entered the house looking for the video game player. While inside, the deceased got into a physical confrontation with Javier's mother who testified that the deceased pulled her hair and appeared to be drunk.

Jose Vidal, the other defendant, pulled the deceased out of the apartment on to the street. The deceased took a box cutter

193

from his pocket and tossed it to someone else on the street. Then, the deceased, apparently to demonstrate how tough or angry he was, banged his head several times on the pole of a street parking sign. Javier, who testified he was arrested wearing sandals, not workboots, saw the deceased fighting with his father on the street and called the police.

Because the injuries to the deceased did not appear to be life threatening, the police did not call the Crime Scene Unit to immediately take photographs of the scene. Photographs of the scene were taken months after the incident by the District Attorney's Office in preparation for trial. Those photographs did not show any street parking sign. This undercut the defense contention that the deceased may have caused his own head injuries when he purportedly intentionally banged his head against the pole. Nevertheless, the defendants were essentially contending that they were justified in hitting the deceased to terminate his attempt to unlawfully enter their home.

I had mentioned that what happened after the incident is what makes this case memorable to me. In contrast to the hospital's negligence, there was the diligence of my court clerk, Erik DeLucca. During a recess in the trial and without telling anyone, out of curiosity, he looked up the crime scene on Google Earth. He found a photograph of the street showing a street parking sign with a pole that was not in the photographs taken by the District Attorney's Office. Apparently for some reason that sign had been removed before the District Attorney's Office photographs were taken.

The Google Earth picture of the street showed painted graffiti on the asphalt in large letters at the exact location of the fight which said, "R.I.P. John" which was first name of the deceased. This graffiti was proof that the Google Earth photograph had been taken after the incident and that there had been a street parking sign there.

After my court clerk showed me what he had found, I alerted the attorneys for both sides to this evidence. The defense downloaded the photograph and, without objection from the prosecution, it was introduced as a defense exhibit at the trial.

The jury found the both defendants not guilty of all charges. I assume their verdict was based on the defense contention that the defendants acted reasonably in defending their home from being entered by the deceased and that the severe injuries to the head of the deceased, in fact, may have been self-inflicted.

In finding the defendants not guilty of the charges involving injury to the deceased based on self-defense, the jury never had to decide the more difficult question of whether the defendants were responsible for causing his death despite the hospital's gross negligence which resulted in septic shock to the deceased.

A MAFIA KILLING AND A WITNESS CHANGES HER STORY

People v. Joseph Watts (343/96 -Richmond County)

This murder trial took place in 1997 in Staten Island where I was assigned to sit in Supreme Court from 1997 to 1999 as an additional trial judge. This assignment was in response to a law suit brought against the Office of Court Administration by an attorney, Duane Felton, concerning the backlog of pending felony cases there. After the backlog was substantially reduced during this assignment, the law suit was dropped, and I was reassigned back to Brooklyn.

I am including a discussion of this trial even though it is outside the period covered by the other trials in this book, not only because it happens to be interesting, but also because it involves two difficult decisions I had to make which I will discuss following a discussion of the trial itself.

Watts was found not guilty at this trial, so the factual summary below is based on the prosecution's contentions at the trial and not on what the jury found to be true. Following his acquittal, Watts was convicted in federal court of various charges involving organized crime activities and received a substantial prison sentence.

This case involved a murder allegedly committed by Watts whom the prosecution contended was a close advisor to the notorious John Gotti, the reputed Mafia leader of the Gambino Crime Family. The prosecution contended that in 1987, in the vicinity of John Gotti's social club in Ozone Park Queens, the Bergen Hunt & Fish Club, William Ciccone, while dressed as a priest, fired a shot at Gotti as he emerged from the club. Ciccone's shot missed, and he was chased down and apprehended by Gotti's associates. Ciccone was then beaten and forced into an automobile.

Watts, who could not become a "made member" of Gotti's Mafia family because he was not Italian, was, nevertheless, a close advisor to Gotti. Watts was summoned by Gotti to see him in Queens to discuss the situation. There, according to the prosecution, Watts was ordered by Gotti to find out if Ciccone was acting on his own or was sent as a hitman by someone, possibly an organized crime rival.

Ciccone was put into the trunk of Watts' car and driven to Staten Island to another social club on Railroad Avenue in the

Dongan Hills neighborhood. There Ciccone was allegedly beaten and tortured with the assistance of two brothers who were also affiliated with organized crime in an effort to get him to reveal who sent him to kill Gotti. After becoming convinced that Ciccone was acting on his own and not sent by anyone, Watts and the two brothers transported Ciccone in a bodybag to a candy store, Paul's Sweet Shop, located on New Dorp Plaza, which was owned by another reputed organized crime member who was related to the two brothers.

Ciccone was taken to the basement. Watts telephoned Gotti and told Gotti that he believed Ciccone was acting on his own. Gotti then ordered Watts to kill Ciccone, which he did by shooting him several times in the head. Watts and the two brothers then left the candy store to get tools in order to dig up the basement's cement floor and bury Ciccone there.

While they were gone, the police were called to the candy store by a passing motorist who saw a door off its hinges and suspected a burglary had taken place there. On arriving and inspecting the premises, the police discovered Ciccone's tortured and shot body in the basement inside the bodybag.

The police Crime Scene Unit investigated the scene, but, at this point, the police had insufficient evidence to arrest anyone. Watts' fingerprint was found on a soda glass on the candy store counter, which an employee had said she had cleaned before the store was closed. But without additional evidence, this fingerprint was insufficient to arrest Watts for the murder.

This additional evidence came almost 10 years later through the testimony of formerly 400 pound, now about 250 pound, Dominic "Fat Dom" Borghese, a member of the Gambino Crime Family. Borghese had pleaded guilty to serious federal charges involving disposing of the bodies of several murdered organized crime victims and was facing a long prison sentence. In return for a shorter sentence and placement in the Witness Protection Program, he agreed to testify in this case and other federal cases.

According to Borghese, Watts borrowed Borghese's truck to move Ciccone from the social club in Dongan Hills to the candy store in New Dorp and later admitted to Borghese that he had shot Ciccone in the basement of the candy store. He also told Borghese when he returned the truck to burn it.

Watts told Borghese that he, Watts, could not return to the store to bury the body, because the police were there and that he had left his fingerprints on one of the soda glasses and possibly on the counter. Watts told Borghese he would get one of the women who worked in the store to say he was a customer in the store before it closed for the evening.

Borghese was vigorously and effectively cross-examined by Watts' lead attorney, Jimmy LaRosa, an excellent trial advocate who had represented many organized crime figures. LaRosa brought out all of the crimes Borghese had admitting to committing when he made his agreement to become a cooperating witness with the federal prosecutors. In addition, LaRosa brought out that at the time of his federal conviction, Borghese claimed to be indigent and unable to pay the $100,000 fine imposed as part of that conviction.

Nevertheless, LaRosa was able to establish that Borghese had about $140,000 hidden in a safe deposit box at a Staten Island bank. During the trial, based on information provided to me in affidavit from by LaRosa, I signed a subpoena to permit a search of that safe deposit box. My law clerk at the time, Charmaine Black, accompanied the attorneys for both sides to the bank and, it was agreed that she would count any money found there. As an example of how thorough LaRosa wanted to be, he also had a videographer and a gemologist accompany the group to the bank to document the proceedings and appraise any jewelry that might be found. No jewelry was found but finding the money in the safe deposit box was enough drama.

The relevance of these hidden funds was that Borghese had agreed as part of his plea arrangement in federal court to be truthful in order to receive the benefits of his plea bargain and reduced sentence. His hiding of these funds established that he was not truthful which would allow the federal prosecutors to request that the federal court void the agreement. According to the defense argument, this gave Borghese an even greater motivation to "please the government" with his testimony.

Further, because Borghese had claimed he was indigent, his wife was receiving a subsidy from the federal prosecutor's for living expenses as part of his plea arrangement, when, in fact, she had access to the funds in the safe deposit box. These funds also were never reported to the IRS.

LaRosa also had obtained the records of Borghese's wife's numerous purchases at Home Shopping Club and QVC which were also inconsistent with his claim that he had no funds at the time he said he could not pay the federal fine. I recall the jurors laughing and shaking their heads as LaRosa itemized some of her purchases. LaRosa also established that Borghese had not declared hundreds of thousands of dollars in his organized crime income from loansharking and bookmaking.

As an aside, Borghese was not the only witness to feel the impact of LaRosa's cross-examination. During the cross-examination of one of the Crime Scene Unit Detectives, LaRosa referred to a series of photographs of the candy store counter showing the soda glass where the fingerprint had been found. Also on the counter was a clear plastic doughnut case containing several doughnuts. LaRosa asked the detective, after establishing that keeping the crime scene free from being altered was important, if any of the police officers there had eaten any of the doughnuts.

When the detective said no, LaRosa asked him to look at the pictures taken by the Crime Scene Unit which had been placed in evidence by the prosecution and see whether the number of doughnuts in the case decreased from picture to picture. When the detective said the pictures did not have close-ups of the case to enable him to count the doughnuts in each picture, LaRosa dramatically pulled from a pocket inside his multi-buttoned, double-breasted, custom-made, suit jacket a very large magnifying glass and handed it to the detective.

In fact, a magnifying glass was not needed to see that the pictures showed different numbers of doughnuts and no one inferred the number was going up rather than down. This testimony, to some extent, may have undermined the testimony concerning the integrity of the fingerprint on the soda glass which was on the same counter as the doughnut case.

More critically, the candy store employee who told the police when the fingerprint was found that she cleared the counter before closing the store that night, testified at the trial that there were times when she did not completely clear the counter, and that night may have been one of them. She also testified that Watts was a customer in the store that day, which would provide an innocent explanation why his fingerprint was on the soda glass.

Borghese, by providing his truck, could be considered an "accomplice" in the kidnapping if not also the murder of Ciccone, if he provided his truck to Watts knowing that Watts would be using the truck for an illegal purpose. Under New York law, Watts could not be convicted solely on the testimony of an accomplice without "other evidence tending to connect" Watts to the crime. This "other evidence" was the fingerprint on the soda glass. However, when the store employee testified that the soda glass may have been placed on the counter by Watts while the store was open for business, the case was effectively destroyed.

In my experience, there is naturally a "fear factor" when jurors are hearing an organized crime case. Indeed, it was very difficult to even find jurors willing to sit on this case once jurors were informed by me during preliminary screening of potential jurors with the attorneys present that the case involved a murder allegedly committed at the request of John Gotti.

When the victim is also involved in organized crime, as many victims in these cases are, or can be regarded as "bringing it upon himself," as clearly was the situation with Ciccone, who according to the prosecution's own case started it all by taking a shot a John Gotti, jurors, from my experience in other cases, require proof of guilt far above and beyond what would suffice in a different type of case to overcome the "fear factor" posed by a defendant allegedly affiliated with organized crime

About a week prior to the date scheduled to begin jury selection in this case, I received information from court security personnel who had been alerted by the police department, that a prisoner being held in Rikers Island who was due to be released soon, had told Watts, who was also confined there, that if Watts' upcoming trial was not going well, he would kill one of the jurors. Even though many years have passed, I will not further discuss the source of this information.

To address this issue, a meeting was held between me and court security personnel. I was given the option of having the selected jurors kept in a hotel under guard by court officers for the duration of the trial which was expected to last at least four weeks. At the time of this trial, juries were routinely sequestered in a hotel once deliberations had started, but it was almost unheard of to sequester juries during the trial itself.

The jury in the O.J. Simpson murder trial in Los Angeles two years before was fully sequestered to shield them from the media accounts of the trial. Finding jurors willing and able not to work or go home for a month involves selecting people whose personal lives are different from most people and results in a group of jurors who, to put it politely, may not be best suited to concentrate on a lengthy case. That might explain the shamefully quick verdict in the Simpson case, and I wanted no part of that experience in this trial.

I evaluated the likelihood of that threat actually being carried out by the person who made the threat. He had no known background in this type of crime. I also believed that Watts was too smart to get involved with this person, who was not part of his select group of associates. Therefore, I decided that the jury would not be sequestered during the trial and that the extra high level of court security that was proposed as an alternative would be sufficient.

This person did show up in the courtroom for one day during the trial which created a bit of a stir among the court officers who all were given his picture so they could be aware if he did show up, but nothing came of it.

Prior to trial, the prosecution made a motion that there be an "anonymous jury," with neither side knowing the names and home addresses of the jurors. This type of motion is made where there is a fear of jury tampering by the defense, or where there is a fear for the safety of the jurors either during or after the trial. In this case, the prosecution made its request based on a fear that the defendant, through his alleged organized crime associates, would attempt to tamper with one or more jurors.

This type of motion is often made in organized crime cases or terrorism cases tried in federal court. The prosecution could not cite any prior New York state court case granting such a motion. I wrote a decision denying the prosecution's motion based on a New York statute which allows a court to deny public disclosure of jurors' addresses "except to counsel for either party" where there is a likelihood of bribery, jury, tampering, or physical injury to a juror. Even this statute did not give the court the authority to deny disclosure of a juror's name nor the authority to deny the juror's address to the attorneys in the case.

My decision noted that if the prosecution could show some evidence that Watts had actually done something to indicate that he, or someone acting on his behalf, would tamper with the jury, then I would consider granting the motion. The decision also urged the Legislature to consider amending the statute to give a trial court more discretion to select an anonymous jury. To date, the statute has not been changed, and I am not aware of any case where an anonymous jury has been selected in a New York State court over the objection of a defendant.

The second thing that is not generally known about this case is that about two weeks after the acquittal, I was called into the office of the long-serving and highly regarded Supervising Judge of the Staten Island Supreme Court, Wally Sangiorgio. He told me that he, myself, and Court of Appeals Judge Vito J. Titone had been invited by Jimmy LaRosa to join him and the two other defense attorney's involved in the trial, Paul LeMole, then regarded as the dean of the Staten Island criminal bar, and LaRosa's associate, Andrew J. Weinstein, for dinner at one of the best Italian restaurants on Staten Island.

I told Judge Sangiorgio that I felt awkward about doing this, but I was assured that his presence and the presence of Judge Titone would be clear evidence that there would be no appearance of impropriety in accepting the invitation. I accepted the invitation, and, I must say, it was a very pleasant evening.

About three years later, after I had been transferred back to Brooklyn, I was called into the chambers of the Brooklyn Administrative Judge and asked if I had gone out to dinner with Jimmy LaRosa after the acquittal in the Watts case. Evidently, someone had made a comment about this to someone in the Court Administration, and the Administrative Judge in Brooklyn was told to now ask me about this, even though several years had passed. I said I had done so only because I was accompanied by the Supervising Judge from Staten Island, who was my supervisor at the time, and a sitting judge on the New York Court of Appeals, and, if I had refused, they might have been upset with me. I heard nothing more about the matter.

PART III. ADDITIONAL RECOLLECTIONS

Chapter 18. *"THE BEST MAN IS NOT ALLOWED NEW JERSEY"*

By virtue of being a judge in New York and filing a form with the City Clerk, I was permitted to solemnize marriages which I occasionally did at the request of people I knew. When a friend asked me to officiate at his daughter's wedding, it was my pleasure to agree to do so. I was told that the ceremony and the reception was to be held on a boat cruising New York harbor which made me even more willing to do so.

When I met with the prospective bride and groom a few weeks before the wedding to go over the details of the ceremony and ask their preferences about the different ways it could be done, I told them that the wedding had to take place within the borders of New York State, because my New York State judicial office did not give me the authority to perform marriages outside of New York.

The wedding invitation had specified that the boat would be leaving from Chelsea Piers on the West Side of Manhattan. Therefore, I told them that we and their two witnesses would sign the marriage license while the boat was docked there, and I would put the address of Chelsea Piers on the license as the location where the wedding took place.

After the wedding ceremony was completed, this license form had to be filed with the City Clerk and contain the "mailing address" where the wedding was performed. Placing the address of Chelsea Piers on the license as the location of the wedding made a lot more sense than putting the map coordinates of New York harbor on the license and would avoid the almost certain bureaucratic hassles that would otherwise result when the license was filed.

I also checked a map and determined that in New York harbor, the boundary between New York and New Jersey was an imaginary line approximately between the southern tip of Manhattan and the center of the Verrazano Bridge. Therefore, I told the prospective bride and groom that at the time of the actual ceremony, I would like the boat to be on the New York side of that line. They understood and agreed.

But a week before the wedding, all of the invitees received a mailed note that the boat would not be leaving from Chelsea Piers. Instead, it would depart from Weehawken, New Jersey, because the parking lots there were more accommodating. Anticipating a real problem with the marriage license, I called the bride and explained the need to have a New York address for the wedding.

She said, not to worry, because after leaving Weehawken, the boat would be going to Chelsea Piers to pick up the best man. When I asked her why, she said, "The best man is not allowed in New Jersey."

I mulled this over for a few seconds, and, realizing that states do not have the power to banish people, I asked if the reason was that the best man was not allowed to leave New York because he was on probation or on parole from jail. She said, he had been convicted of a white collar crime involving some kind of stock fraud. As a result, he was on probation and could not leave New York State as a condition of his probation.

In the end, it all worked out. We picked up the best man at Chelsea Piers and signed the license there. He seemed like a very nice fellow.

Chapter 19. *A COURTROOM JOKE BACKFIRES*

This recollection, as well as the following one, concerns courtroom incidents in which I was involved as an Assistant District Attorney. Both involved the same Supreme Court trial judge, who was very intelligent and exceptionally hardworking. However, in each of these incidents, he took a judicial action that was inappropriate. Although no permanent harm resulted, these incidents illustrate how quickly things can go bad for a judge who does not think things through before taking a judicial action.

Even though the judge is now deceased, I do not feel comfortable using his name here, because I am not also discussing his many admirable qualities. Therefore, I will call him "Judge Cherry."

Judge Cherry was trying a robbery case where the defendant had been arrested seven months after the robbery when the victim saw the defendant on the street. The victim believed the defendant was the person who had robbed him and called the police who arrested the defendant. The defendant asserted that he was mistakenly identified and claimed, as an alibi, that at the time of the robbery he was in a locked psychiatric ward in Creedmore Psychiatric Center in Queens. Nevertheless, the defendant was indicted and the case went to trial.

In an effort to refute the defendant's alibi, the prosecution attempted to call a television news reporter, John Johnson of WABC in New York, who had done a series of stories on the lax security conditions at Creedmore. However, lawyers from WABC persuaded Judge Cherry that John Johnson should not be compelled by subpoena to testify at this trial. The prosecution, as a result, rested its case without presenting any witnesses to refute the

Creedmore records showing the defendant was confined there at the time of the robbery.

The next morning when summations were scheduled, Judge Cherry, apparently in the friendly spirit that existed during the trial among the attorneys and the judge, suggested to the prosecutor that when the defense attorney arrived in court, that the prosecutor announce that he had discovered five surprise witnesses from Creedmore to testify that the defendant was not in Creedmore at the time of the robbery.

When the defense attorney arrived, the defendant, who was out on bail, had not yet arrived. The court stenographer was also in on the joke and agreed to pretend to transcribe the proceedings. With the defendant not present, the prosecutor made the bogus application as suggested by the judge to call five surprise witnesses to rebut the defendant's alibi. Defense counsel strongly objected to allowing the prosecutor to call these witnesses and argued that the prosecutor had not given the pre-trial notice of an intent to call these witnesses as specifically required by New York's Criminal Procedure Law.

Judge Cherry then interrupted defense counsel and told him to relax, because the prosecutor was only joking. Defense counsel did not indicate he was upset. When the defendant arrived, defense counsel gave his summation. The trial then recessed for lunch with the prosecutor's summation to follow.

When the trial reconvened after lunch, the courtroom was filled with defense counsel's colleagues from the Legal Aid Society. It was common knowledge that Judge Cherrry was not popular with many of the attorneys from the Legal Aid Society because of his perceived "pro-prosecution" bias.

Defense counsel complained to Judge Cherry that the morning's bogus application by the prosecutor had "unnerved" him and caused him to give a less than effective summation. Defense counsel then asked for a mistrial, because he believed the defendant's case had been adversely affected.

Judge Cherry was surprised and, no doubt, embarrassed. He granted the request for a mistrial "to avoid the appearance of wrong-doing," and set a date for the retrial to begin. He denied the defense request to disqualify himself from presiding over the retrial.

Three days before the retrial was to begin, the defendant brought a proceeding in the Appellate Division to bar the retrial and dismiss the indictment on the grounds that principles of Double Jeopardy would bar a retrial. The defense argued that even though the mistrial was requested by the defendant which ordinarily would permit a second trial, the mistrial request was triggered by improper judicial and prosecutorial misconduct which was either intended to provoke a mistrial request by the defense or was the result of gross negligence for failing to perceive that the defense would request a mistrial as a result of the bogus proceedings.

This is where I came into the case as Deputy Chief of the Appeals Bureau. Someone alerted the local newspapers to what Judge Cherry had done, and there were articles that were embarrassing both to him and the District Attorney's Office. It was, therefore, important to the District Attorney's Office that, despite the inappropriate conduct, that the case not be dismissed based on the Double Jeopardy claim, which implied a nefarious purpose was behind the joke, and, to the extent possible, that it be made known that what had occurred in the courtroom was actually in the context of the parties' informal and friendly relationship that had existed during the trial.

The Appellate Division denied the Double Jeopardy claim, finding, that, in fact, the defendant clearly was not prejudiced by the conduct "which must be deplored." In fact, during the oral argument of the case before the Appellate Division, one of the Justices (the very same J. Irwin Shapiro to whom years before I had apologized for not knowing the meaning of the phrase "withdrawal of a juror") commented that it appeared that defense counsel did not complain about the incident until "someone put a bug in his ear." The Appellate Division permitted a retrial but ordered that it be held before a different Judge.

The New York Court of Appeals denied the defense permission to appeal to that Court. Because the defendant was claiming a violation of the Double Jeopardy Clause of the United States Constitution, he was procedurally permitted to bring a new proceeding in federal court to bar the retrial of the case. His petition in the United States District Court for the Eastern District of New York was denied by a federal judge who also found the claim that defense counsel's summation was impaired by the joke to be without merit.

Finally, the case was appealed to the United States Court of Appeals for the Second Circuit where I had to argue this case before a panel of three judges that included Judge Irving Kaufman, best known for having sentenced Julius and Ethel Rosenberg to death when he presided over their espionage trial in the 1950's. Not surprisingly, he found no humor in Judge Cherry's joke, but he and the other two judges on that panel also found that the Double Jeopardy claim was without merit.

One lesson to be learned from this unfortunate judicial lapse of judgment, is that nothing is guaranteed to be "off the record" with some attorneys, so a judge should always speak and act accordingly. Personally, when I was tempted to make a humorous "off the record" remark from the bench that might be interpreted the wrong way, I would whisper it to the court reporter, a court officer, or my court clerk. They could always be trusted to smile and keep it to themselves.

Chapter 20. *A SUGGESTED "PRISONER EXCHANGE"*

A few years after the Judge Cherry joke case was resolved, another incident in his courtroom took place that also resulted in my becoming involved in the situation. When the prosecutor assigned to a manslaughter case told the judge that the prosecution needed an adjournment to find an important witness, the judge wanted the prosecutor to put on the record in open court the efforts being made to find the witness.

Because these details would have revealed the possible whereabouts of the witness to the defense, the prosecutor requested to give this information to the judge in private. A sealed record of this information would have been made for future use by an appellate court if needed. However, the judge insisted that this information be made public and summoned the prosecutor's Supreme Court Bureau Chief, Alan Trachtman, to his courtroom to discuss the issue. On arriving, Mr. Trachtman respectfully refused to publicly disclose this information out of concern for jeopardizing the safety of the witness. Mr. Trachtman's concern was not unrealistic. Not too long before, a judge in Manhattan had ordered that a police report containing the address of a witness be turned over to the defense over the objection of the prosecutor in that case, and, shortly after, the witness was murdered. Judge Cherry warned Mr. Trachtman that he would hold him in contempt and immediately jail him if he persisted in his refusal. Apparently, Judge Cherry believed Mr. Trachtman would back down upon the threat of being incarcerated, but when Mr. Trachtman held firm, the judge carried out his threat and ordered that Mr. Trachtman be confined to an empty jury deliberation room in the custody of a court officer.

The Office was notified of Mr. Trachtman's situation, and I was dispatched to resolve it. At the time, I was the First Deputy

Bureau Chief of the Supreme Court Bureau, having been reassigned out of the Appeals Bureau several years before, and Mr. Trachtman was my immediate supervisor. I knew I had to de-escalate the situation. I also knew that his summarily holding Mr. Trachtman in contempt was not authorized, because there was no immediate need to restore order to the courtroom or publicly reveal the information Judge Cherry was demanding. Mr. Trachtman would have been entitled to a hearing before another judge to determine whether he was actually in contempt of court for willfully disobeying a lawful order. But this was not the time to raise these technicalities with Judge Cherry.

I had maintained a cordial relationship with Judge Cherry both during and after the litigation concerning the joke incident, and I was going to rely on that. When I arrived in his courtroom, I told the judge that Mr. Trachtman was very important to the Office and that we were willing to exchange a lower level supervisor, Ned Fox, who directly supervised the prosecutors appearing before Judge Cherry for Mr. Trachtman. I believed I could get away with this absurd proposition to "exchange prisoners" based on my prior relationship with Judge Cherry. He smiled. The tension in the courtroom was relieved. Mr. Trachtman was immediately released, and the judge, perhaps as a result of a telephone call from the Administrative Judge of the Supreme Court, no longer demanded that the information be made public. Mr. Trachtman, being a good lawyer, not to mention a loyal soldier who was willing to go to jail to protect the witness's safety, asked Judge Cherry to expunge the record of the so-called contempt proceeding. The judge granted the request. To be certain that the record was "expunged," Mr. Trachtman actually ordered the minutes of the proceedings from the court reporter to insure that the pages were blank.

Chapter 21. *MIDNIGHT IN THE GARDEN OF GOOD AND EVIL*

When a new person joins an organization that has a rotating schedule of assignments, it is almost universally expected that the newcomer will get the least desirable dates to work. This is logically based on the assumption that the existing staff has already worked its share of those dates. Well, when I became a judge in July of 1987, the schedule-makers had me in their sights when they arranged the schedule for the rest of that year.

My first assignment was to the Criminal Court in Queens where I was assigned to what was known as an "All Purpose Part" or "AP Part," for short. A case came into an AP Part after the defendant's arraignment following the arrest. Judges in AP Parts were responsible for holding conferences on the cases to see if there would be a guilty plea, supervising the disclosure of information about the case that was required to be given by the prosecution, and expediting the parties' readiness to go to trial. Routine judicial decisions had to be made in every case, and this was an excellent way for a new judge to learn the ropes in Criminal Court, a place where I had not handled cases for 16 years.

Criminal Court Judges in Queens also had responsibility for sitting in Night Court Arraignments, which operated from 5:00 pm to 1:00 am. In New York, defendants are entitled to be arraigned within 24 hours of their arrest. To even come close to meeting this requirement due to the daily volume of arrests, Criminal Court arraignment parts in each New York City county had a Night Court session, with the exception of Staten Island where the arrest volume could be handled during the day session.

The Night Court assignment in Queens was for seven nights from Monday through Sunday. To compensate for working seven consecutive nights, a Judge was given the following Monday and

214

Tuesday off. Soon after beginning my assignment in Queens, I was told that I would be assigned to work Night Court in Queens Christmas week, after which I would be transferred to sit in Criminal Court in Brooklyn.

Although I enjoyed working with the judges in the Queens Criminal Court, many of whom were extremely helpful to me in answering my many questions and giving me sound advice, I looked forward to being transferred back to Brooklyn. It was the general policy of the Court Administration to not immediately assign someone who had just left a prosecutor's office to sit as a Criminal Court Judge in the same county. There was too much of a chance that the new judge would have had some role as a prosecutor in a case that would come before the new judge. I did not expect to be transferred to Brooklyn for at least a year, so the thought of the impending Brooklyn transfer made working Night Court Christmas week something I actually looked forward to doing.

Shortly after being advised of the Queens Night Court assignment, which would end 1:00 am on December 28, 1987, I was informed of another even less desirable assignment, which was to handle arraignments in the "Lobster Shift" in Manhattan the following week for four nights beginning 1:00 am on January 1, 1988.

The Lobster Shift, as it was called, existed only in Manhattan due to the exceptional volume of arrests there. Cases calendared for the Lobster Shift consisted mostly of minor "quality of life" offenses and victimless crimes, such as loitering in the Port Authority bus terminal, loitering for purposes of prostitution in various neighborhoods in Manhattan, unlicensed peddling, possession of small amounts of drugs, and various con games directed at tourists in the Times Square area. The shift followed the Night Court session and was from 1:00 am to 9:00 am.

The assignment, originally for seven days, then four days, and later three days, was rotated among the over 100 Criminal Court Judges sitting in New York City, so the assignment would come about once every two years. In the 1990's, the Lobster Shift was mercifully abolished. The closing was attributed to some combination of budget reasons and the refusal of the long-serving Manhattan District Attorney, Robert Morganthau, who was immune from public criticism, to provide prosecutors to work that shift.

The Lobster Shift schedule-makers, like the Queens Night Court schedule-makers, kept the undesirable weeks reserved for new judges, and, thus, I worked these undesirable shifts back-to-back during the so-called "holiday season." But this was all new to me, so the excitement of the experience got me through those two weeks. To add to the excitement, on the afternoon of December 31st before reporting for my first night of the Lobster Shift, I received a call from the Supervising Judge of the Manhattan Criminal Court giving me a heads up that a reporter from the New York Times, Sarah Lyall, had been given permission to sit next to me on the bench that night to do a story about what the ensuing January 2, 1988 article called "the most undesirable court session of the year." In reading the article that morning, I learned that my Lobster Shift was the first time court officials decided to have a Lobster Shift on January first, rather than closing the court session in deference to the holiday. Lucky me. While sitting next to me on the bench, the reporter interviewed me during the brief breaks between the calling of the next case. The article also said that I did not appear to get sleepy as the night wore on and that I kept myself fortified with the thermos of strong coffee I had brought from home.

I still remember the feeling I had driving to Manhattan that night as 1987 was turning to 1988. As I said to the reporter, "I drove past City Hall and the building where I was sworn in. What a way to ring in the New Year. I was thrilled."

One more thing about that night. The photographer who accompanied the reporter decided to leave before I took the bench. No one wanted to be there if they didn't have to. He had taken the picture of the judge who worked the Night Court shift before me, my colleague, Judge Michael A. Gary. That's why the Times article about me is accompanied by his picture. Judge Gary looks very judicious in the photograph, so if people were under the misimpression that it was a picture of me, that was fine as far as I was concerned.

Chapter 22. *IS MY CAR READY?*

There are situations where a judge has discretion whether to excuse himself if he personally knows the defendant, and should do so if he believes he cannot be fair. I found myself thinking about this late one Friday afternoon in 1990. I was sitting as the Arraignment Judge in Brooklyn Criminal Court. I was probably the only judge remaining in the courthouse when the case of a defendant who had been arrested the day before for intoxicated driving was called to be arraigned on the charges. I recognized the name and the face. It was my neighbor who lived up the street from me on Staten Island. He owned a gas station. He also, unfortunately, had a drinking problem. According to the court papers which I quickly scanned, he was driving from Brooklyn to Manhattan via the Battery Tunnel when he was stopped at the toll booth by an officer who believed he was intoxicated by his display of erratic driving, bloodshot eyes, and the odor of alcohol on his breath.

Breath tests later administered by the police confirmed that he had over the legal amount of alcohol in his blood, and he was arrested. Fortunately, no one was injured. I later learned when I spoke with him after I was no longer the judge on the case that he was returning a car that had been repaired at his gas station to the car's owner who was in Manhattan. My dilemma that afternoon was that if I declined to handle the arraignment because I knew the defendant, he would have to remain incarcerated for several more hours until the case was called in Night Court. I asked the prosecutor and the defendant's attorney from the Legal Aid Society to approach the bench. Although the defendant could afford an attorney, he did not have an opportunity to retain one, so the Legal Aid Society was representing him just for the arraignment. I could have disclosed to the attorneys that I knew the defendant. This disclosure would allow either of them, if they wished, to make a record that they had no objection to me handling the case or, alternatively, request that I "recuse" myself. However, I would not be required to recuse myself if I believed my knowing the defendant would have no bearing on my ability to be fair and impartial.

I decided not to disclose that knew the defendant, because my involvement would be just for this one arraignment of a routine case where the defendant, who had no prior criminal record and who was a home and business owner, was not a likely candidate to have bail set on him by any judge. At the bench conference, I asked the prosecutor if he was planning to ask for bail in the case without telling him I knew the defendant. The prosecutor said he was planning on consenting to the defendant's release without bail. Therefore, the only thing I had to decide would be the next court date. If the prosecutor had said he would be requesting bail, I would have recused myself, because my impartiality in making a bail decision might reasonably be questioned. But because no bail was being requested and there would be no discussions about a guilty plea until the defendant had his own attorney, I believed there would be no point in raising the issue about me knowing the defendant and having it placed on the record. The attorneys returned to their positions. The arraignment proceeded in the usual fashion with the defendant being released and given a date to come back to the courthouse with an attorney.

There was one other thing I did not mention to the attorneys. At the time, my car was in the defendant's gas station for routine servicing. I had driven my wife's car to work, and we were planning on picking my car up from the defendant's garage when I got home. I did not see the point of recusing myself from the defendant's arraignment and having him wait in the holding cells until he could be released in Night Court just because he was unlucky enough to have me both as his judge and as his customer. The bottom line, to me, is that justice was served by my silence. And yes, I paid the full repair bill.

Chapter 23. *KUNSTLER PUTS ON A SHOW*

William Kunstler was a nationally famous civil rights attorney whose celebrated clients included the Freedom Riders, the Chicago Seven, the Black Panthers, the Weather Underground, and the American Indian Movement, to name only a few. In February of 1978, he represented Joan Little in an extradition proceeding in Brooklyn where he was opposing the return of Joan Little to North Carolina where she was charged with escaping from prison.

Joan Little was also nationally famous at the time. After a string of theft arrests and convictions in North Carolina in the early 1970's, she was convicted in 1974 of a burglary charge. While imprisoned, she escaped after stabbing a prison guard in the head and heart with an ice pick. The guard's body was found in her prison cell on her bed, naked from the waist down. His semen was found on his bare leg.

She turned herself in about a week later and said she had killed the guard in self-defense, because the guard was sexually assaulting her while threatening her with the ice pick. He had put the ice pick down, she said, when she was being forced to give him oral sex while he was sitting on her bed. It was during this act, that she was able to get her hands on the ice pick and stab him.

In 1975, Little was tried for murder and facing a mandatory death sentence if convicted. The case attracted national attention, particularly from death penalty opponents, feminists, and civil rights advocates due to the racial component in the case, being that she was Black and the guard was White. At trial, she claimed she was defending herself from a sexual attack, while the prosecution claimed she had seduced the guard in order to escape. She was acquitted by a jury.

She still had time remaining to serve on her original sentence. In October of 1977, about one month before she was eligible to be paroled, she was out of prison on a work release program and did not return. In December of 1977, she was arrested in Brooklyn after a 70 mile per hour car chase through Brooklyn streets. An extradition process mostly involving paperwork began, resulting in New York Governor Hugh Carey signing a warrant for her to be returned to North Carolina.

Following the signing of the warrant, there was an extradition proceeding in February of 1978 in Brooklyn Supreme Court before Justice Leonard Scholnick. I was then Deputy Chief of the Appeals Bureau and represented the Brooklyn District Attorney's Office at that proceeding. There were two prosecutors from North Carolina present to observe the proceedings and supply information to the Court if needed. William Kunstler was representing Joan Little.

Led by community activists, there were scores of demonstrators outside the courthouse protesting the extradition and dozens more inside Judge Scholnick's courtroom. The atmosphere was highly charged.

Prior to the case being called, all the parties met with Judge Scholnick in an ante-room outside the main courtroom. The judge and Kunstler first exchanged memories of a law course that Kunstler had taught and in which the judge had been a student. Kunstler then told the judge that he was going to argue that the judge should not grant the extradition request, because he claimed that Joan Little's life would be in danger from prison guards seeking revenge against her if she were returned to the North Carolina prison system. The judge said he would not grant that request and that Kunstler should bring a proceeding in North Carolina to have Little released or given special protection if he could prove that her life would be in danger while in jail there. Kunstler said he understood and asked the judge to delay his extradition order, called a "stay," until he could appeal the extradition order. The judge said he would do that, and everyone was in agreement.

As we all arose to go into the courtroom, Kunstler asked us to wait a moment. He removed his wristwatch, and from his pocket he took out another watch which had a large beaded wristband with six-inch strings of Indian beads hanging down from it. The wristband was clearly in an American Indian style and, no doubt, connected to the American Indian Movement and the trials of activists Russell Means and Dennis Banks he had been involved with. To those who looked at Kunstler as a publicity hound, this costume change would have helped prove their point. Once in the courtroom, Kunstler had his audience and was prepared to play to it. Despite knowing in advance that all parties had agreed that Judge Scholnick would grant the extradition request and stay his extradition order to give Little an opportunity to appeal this decision, Kunstler, nevertheless, while waiving his Indian-beaded wristband for all to see, made an impassioned plea to Judge Scholnick to deny the extradition request raising the argument that to extradite her would be tantamount to sentencing her to death at the hands of North Carolina prison guards (notwithstanding that after her murder acquittal in North Carolina she had remained in the North Carolina prison system and had been on a work release program when she decided not to return after one of her release dates). After Judge Scholnick denied Kunstler's request to deny extradition or hold a hearing on Kunstler's claims of danger to Little in North Carolina, Kunstler said, "Judge, you gotta give me a stay so I can appeal, I'm begging you," rather than simply asking for the stay knowing in advance that it would be granted. As Kunstler made another impassioned argument while again waiving his Indian-beaded wristband, the courtroom audience, already hearing Kunstler's claims that extradition would be tantamount to death sentence, began to chant, "Give her a stay. Give her a stay."

The judge quickly granted this request, not wishing to allow Kunstler to go on any further in front of the large audience that had now become angry and disturbed after hearing Kunstler's unnecessary emotional pleas that would have made no difference in the court's decisions. After several months of unsuccessful appeals of Judge Scholnick's extradition order, Little was returned to North Carolina. She was convicted there of escape for not returning from her work release program. Kunstler's claims of life-endangering retribution from prison guards never materialized. Little was safely released from prison in North Carolina in June of 1979, about a year after being returned there. The most dangerous moment in this case actually occurred during Kunstler's playing to the audience during the Brooklyn extradition proceeding.

AFTERWORD

My intention in writing this book was not only to capture some of the memorable events of my years as an Assistant District Attorney and a Judge. I also wanted to convey to those possibly interested in a career in criminal law, some of the aspects of trial and appellate practice within the context of real cases and show how interesting and important this work can be, whether on the side of the prosecution or the defense. Certainly, I hope this book will also have some educational and entertainment value to those who want to get a better idea of the variety of cases that go to trial and how the small details of a case often make the difference between conviction and acquittal. Finally, I also hope that the reader will gain a sense of appreciation for the hard work and professionalism that routinely goes into the prosecution and defense of these cases every day. Just multiply the cases in this book by several thousand, and the reader will have some sense of how many people have participated in this process over the last 45 years along with me: dedicated and selfless police officers and detectives; talented and genuinely committed prosecutors and defense attorneys; professional and team oriented court officers, court clerks, and court stenographers; concerned and devoted judges; and jurors who gave their best efforts to reach just verdicts.

I am acutely aware of the many issues in the criminal justice system that I have not discussed in this book, including complaints of inherent racism in the system, mass incarceration as the result of unfair mandatory sentencing laws and plea bargaining restrictions, wrongful convictions as the result of prosecutorial misconduct and inadequate defense counsel, and an unfair bail system that results in unnecessary pre-trial detention of indigent defendants. Those subjects are important, but they were beyond the scope of what I wished to write about.

Perhaps in some small way, this book will create more of a public interest in the criminal justice system and lead to an examination of all the issues in the system that can be improved. While I was part of it, I tried my best to do so.